European Council c

Information Literacy
in Action

Carol Gordon

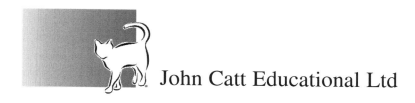

John Catt Educational Ltd

First Published 2000 by John Catt Educational Ltd,
This edition published 2007 by John Catt Educational Ltd,
Great Glemham, Saxmundham, Suffolk IP17 2DH.
Tel: +44 01728 663666   Fax: +44 01728 663415.
E–mail: enqiries@johncatt.co.uk   Internet: http://www.johncatt.com

Opinions expressed in this publication are those of the contributors, and are not necessarily
those of the publishers or the sponsors. We cannot accept responsibility for any errors or
omissions.

The Sex Discrimination Act 1975. The publishers have taken all reasonable steps to avoid a
contravention of Section 38 of the Sex Discrimination Act 1975. However, it should be
noted that (save where there is an express provision to the contrary) where words have been
used which denote the masculine gender only, they shall, pursuant and subject to the said
Act, for the purpose of this publication, be deemed to include the feminine gender and *vice
versa*.

A CIP catalogue record for this book is available from the British Library.

ISBN: 0 901577 57 X

Designed and typeset by John Catt Educational Limited,
Great Glemham, Saxmundham, Suffolk IP17 2DH.

Printed and bound by CPI Antony Rowe, Eastbourne.

Contents

Foreword, *Kevin Bartlett* 5

Preface, *Carolyn Markuson* 6

Introduction, *Carol Gordon* 8

Chapter 1
Learning the Language of the Library 15
    a. Locating and retrieving information (Grades 3-8)
    b. Location and retrieval of library materials (Grades 6-9)
    c. Reading the library shelves (Grades 6-9)
    d. Building a library vocabulary (Grades 2-8)

Chapter 2
Taking Note of History 35
    Evaluating information and sources (Grades 4-7)

Chapter 3
Following the Path of Spiralling Resources 59
    Using print and electronic resources (Grades 6-8)

Chapter 4
Survival Strategies for Reading Non-fiction Text 83
    Reading for understanding (Grades 4-9)

Chapter 5
Looking for the Smoking Gun 91
    Collecting information/data; analysis (Grades 8-10)

Chapter 6
Top Secret: A Search and Detect Mission of Analysis 109
    Display and analysis of information (Grades 5-9)

Chapter 7
Students as Authentic Researchers: Upgrading the Research Paper . . 135
    Establishing focus, gathering data, analysing data (Grades 10-12)

Chapter 8
Putting the Learner in Charge: Is Information Literacy Enough? . . . 169
    Personal management; organisational skills (Grades 9-10)

Chapter 9
Buckets of Books 191
    a. Reading for pleasure (Grades 5-10)
    b. Reading for interpretation and appreciation (Grades 5-10)
    c. Reading for understanding and interpretation (Grades 5-10)
    d. Reading for enjoyment (Grades 5-10)

Foreword: Effective International Schools Series

ECIS is a not for-profit organisation dedicated to the advancement of internationalism through education by the provision of services to its members.

ECIS member schools are spread around the globe and are immensely varied in nature. Yet any of them, new or established, large or small, day or boarding, co-educational or single sex, monocultural or multicultural, can aspire to developing internationally-minded students. The sole proviso as expressed in the ECIS Statement of Philosophy, is that they are committed to the promotion of an international outlook amongst all members of their communities.

ECIS sees its role as providing services, which actively assist schools in working towards this ideal, through practical support. The Effective International Schools series is one way of doing this.

For the purposes of this series, ECIS will restrict itself to those areas of a school's operation with regard to which the Council is in a position to offer sound practical support in the form of documents which offer reliable guidelines and proven examples of good practice. There is much to be gained from sharing the experiences of member schools and little to be gained from reinventing the wheel. Much has been learned since the Council was founded and time, energy and money are too precious to waste. The experience of other schools may offer a real head start.

Each publication will, therefore, have the following elements in common:

- They are driven by a common set of beliefs and values about student learning with an international outlook.

- They are structured so as to illustrate a logical progression from profile to policy to practice.

- They are based on successful experience in international schools, but offer suggestions generic enough to apply in a variety of contexts.

ECIS trusts this series will prove useful to members and welcomes any suggestions for improvements to each publication or for additions to the series.

Kevin Bartlett is Director of Windhoek International School, Namibia

Preface

It is exciting to find groundbreaking thinking that so clearly defines the role of the library in information literacy – and the role of the librarian as collaborator to the instructional process! Carol Gordon is not simply repackaging old lesson plans under new guises, but focuses on taking advantage of what we know about learning and today's children and the challenge of helping them become truly information literate.

Since the times of Plato, we have known how to teach yet we rarely do it and have become almost obsessed with what (topics, disciplines, *etc*) we teach! The recent research on how children learn, recall, and apply higher level thinking skills, has served to reinforce and reiterate what we have long known – how to teach. The time has come to talk about it no longer, but to do it! The tools are in place; the teaching strategies that involve inquiry and authentic experiences are being encouraged if not mandated, and the sheer volume of information requires students and librarians to evaluate carefully and assess its value and accuracy. Our students, born just a few years ago, do not have the same frames of reference we have had. An entertaining yearly list of these differences is compiled by Beloit College in Wisconsin to remind teachers that the children in front of them today are not the same ones that were there 10 or 15 years ago – and these students need a different knowledge base than ours as they live and learn in the future.

Information has, at the risk of being trite, truly become the coin of the realm. The process of information acquisition has taken on far more complex nuances as we involve students in experiences that require them to assess what information they know, what they need to know, where they can look for it, how much of it they need or want, and how accurate the information is. All of this is embedded in the authentic experiences Carol Gordon has provided – experiences that students not only enjoy, but in relevant situations that enable them to connect learning to life. In the past, relevance was defined as a topical issue; today relevance is defined as the connection between learning and life's practices.

This book provides several creatively designed and classroom-tested information literacy experiences that are connected to classroom instruction. They elevate the assignment from drudgery to excitement and provide a holistic approach to teaching and learning. They follow the guidelines for 'best practice' and enable the librarian to connect directly with the learning process. They use what students know and build upon it. They thrust students into unique roles that parallel real-life experiences. And, most of all, these examples provide a basis for the integration of all types of information literacy skills and break down the artificial barriers or separations between the electronic (computer) world of information and the print world.

In past experiences, librarians were often disengaged at the data-gathering stages of the research process. In today's paradigm the librarian, as collaborator with the teacher, is part of the process through to its ultimate goal, that of the synthesis of new knowledge. This provides application for all levels of Bloom's taxonomy and recognizes that fact-finding and data-gathering are essential means to an end, but not an end in and of themselves. The questions today are What is to be done with all that information? How do you know it is accurate, believable? What does it all mean? How does it connect? These lessons and units will provide fertile ground for teachers who are struggling to create real-life experiences and performance based assessments of authentic experiences while at the same time crafting comprehensive information literacy learning for their students. The classroom benefits from the library as it is transformed into an exciting learning laboratory; the students learn and practice life-long skills. Gordon has provided an exciting, readable rationale, several classroom proven examples, and defines the dynamic role of the library in the learning process.

Carolyn Markuson
BiblioTECH Corp

Introduction

The illiterate of the twenty-first century will not be those who cannot read and write, but those who cannot learn, unlearn, and relearn...

Alvin Toffler

What we know about learning

What we have learned about learning in the past two decades has revolutionised the way we think about teaching. No longer do we expect students to sit in neat rows with hands folded, eyes riveted on the teacher. No longer is the textbook sufficient as the sole source of information. No longer is a pencil and paper test the only way, or even the best way, to collect evidence of learning. No longer can the four walls of the classroom define the learner's world. Instead, students as active learners, are engaged in 'focused, experiential learning organised around the investigation and resolution of messy, real-world problems' (Torp & Sage, 1998, p.14).

Educational research has led us to these new paradigms based on what we know about learning:

- The learner constructs knowledge, and learning is a process of creating personal meaning from new information and prior knowledge;
- All ages and abilities can think and solve problems;
- Learning isn't necessarily a linear progression of building discrete skills but a complex interaction of what is known and what is applied;
- There is variety in learning styles and types of intelligences and intelligence can be acquired;
- People perform better when they know the goal, see models, and compare their performance to a standard, or benchmark, that describes what 'good' looks like;
- It is important to know when to use knowledge, how to adapt it, and how to manage one's own learning;
- Learning is situational and not readily transferred to other situations;
- Successful learning involves the use of numerous strategies;
- Motivation, effort and self-esteem affect learning and performance;
- Learning is a social process and group work is valuable;
- Learning how to learn and how to assess one's own work is at least as important as getting high grades on pencil and paper tests.

It is a happy circumstance for educators that what we know about learning converges with a technological revolution that customises and tailors teaching practices to support these paradigm shifts. More than a tool for the learner, electronic information delivery and access affects what we teach and how we teach. It affects what is worth knowing and what is worth knowing how to do. It sets a new agenda for educators. Technology, and specifically Internet access, puts 'real' data at our fingertips and it helps us generate our own raw data. In both instances technology can raise the level of learning from the hunt-and-peck activities that characterised early library instruction to investigative activities that challenge learners to be 'authentic researchers'. In this context the computer becomes more than a tool; it is a unique interactive learning environment that increases cognitive processing and the cognitive and social dimensions of learning. Interactivity adds to the motivating capability of computers and enables the potential for higher order thinking when used to solve a problem (Patterson & Smith, 1986).

How what we know has changed how we teach

Any decision we make about what to do in the classroom is a reflection of our mental model of learning. Embracing a progressive and constructivist definition of learning in a technological age, educators now have a rich repertoire of innovative pedagogical strategies that include:

- Project-based learning
- Discovery learning
- Problem-based inquiry learning
- Critical thinking
- Multiple intelligences
- Resource-based learning
- Co-operative learning
- Metacognitive learning
- Interdisciplinary teaching
- Multi-cultural teaching
- Authentic learning and assessment
- Action research and reflective practice

These teaching strategies constitute what is generally accepted as best practice and each one of them is represented in the project work outlined in this book. The most inclusive of these, authentic learning and assessment, incorporates many of these strategies as it requires students to do meaningful tasks and to know what is expected of them and how to achieve it. Each project included in this collection is an authentic learning task, which requires learners to use the tools of the expert. The projects offer opportunities for problem solving and decision making, and for display, presentation and sharing of outcomes. In these interdisciplinary projects learners are expected to apply information to new situations, to use divergent and critical thinking, to actively engage in a variety of tasks, to make choices, to have opportunities for revision, including self or peer evaluation, and to work in groups.

Assessment of the learning tasks is aimed at what escapes conventional grading and testing. Higher order thinking-skills, such as formulating problems, solving complex, multi-step problems, synthesising knowledge, engaging in co-operation and collaboration, communicating clearly, questioning, and evaluating what has been learned, are the targets of authentic assessment measures. Rubrics, journals and portfolios are the instruments used to measure how successfully the learner achieved the standards set forth at the beginning of the project, and to provide continuous feedback for improvement as well as a summative evaluation for a grade.

Action research is highlighted in some of the projects included in this book to demonstrate how the librarian can work with teachers as a reflective practitioner. Students and teachers participate in the collection and analysis of data throughout the project to determine how its design or implementation can be improved. This is a powerful tool that strengthens collaboration and defines the role of the librarian as coordinator, facilitator and leader.

Information literacy and the librarian's agenda

These teaching strategies are a boon to school library programmes, coming at a time when a technological revolution and the Information Age underscore the need for learner-centric teaching. What were known as 'library skills' and 'research skills' and 'study skills' and 'computer skills' now converge as 'information literacy', which has emerged as the overriding issue in library instruction (Irving, 1985). It is described as a need-driven goal which integrates knowledge of tools and resources with skills and exists independently of, but relating to, literacy and computer literacy (Brevik, 1985). Information literacy raises levels of awareness of the knowledge explosion and how information is organised.

As clarified by Milbury (1998), information literacy 'addresses selection of appropriate resources, analysis and evaluation of the information retrieved, the presentation of findings or solution, and the evaluation of both the outcome and the process used' (p. 43). Information literacy exists when students identify the information they need to solve a problem, know how to find and apply information, and can make decisions that move them toward personal enrichment (Joyce, Tinkham & Trainor, 1993).

Information skills, encompassing literacy, learning to learn, library literacy, information literacy, and computer literacy is a broad term incorporating a range of subordinate or prerequisite skills: those associated with reading, writing, searching, retrieving, organising, processing, thinking, analysing, and presenting. They include hundreds of skills that fall into categories such as researching, studying, computing and retrieving information that are integral to thinking skills ranging from recognition, recall and memorising to analysing, synthesising and evaluating. Information skills are synergistic and context-dependent: one skill depends on another, and they are all grounded in the content of academic disciplines. Most importantly, the skills evolve from content-area objectives that are rooted in the major concepts of the subject disciplines themselves. Figure 1 illustrates how content-area objectives power a programme that is need-driven and classroom centred. While information skills drive the library instruction programme, they are not its starting point. They serve instead as touchstones for information literacy, connecting what is happening in the classroom with what can happen in the library and computer lab.

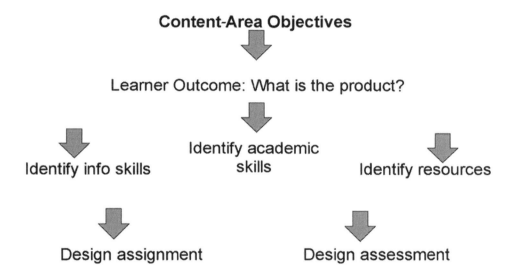

Figure 1: A model for the classroom-library connection.

On the other hand, any standards, or goals, that attempt to describe what we would like learners to know and be able to do must start with the learner. Instruction and curriculum converge as teachers and librarians decide what the learning priorities are. Study and information skills cannot be represented by one curriculum 'area'; they are the substance of all academic work and a great deal of non-academic work in schools (Irving, 1985, p.14).

The process of building strong connections between academic work and information skills is essentially the same whether students are key-word searching in an electronic index or using a print index, *eg* Readers' Guide. The point is that learners are doing meaningful work using information skills while crossing curricular boundaries. Assignments, then are student-centred, interdisciplinary, authentic tasks that are project-based and authentically assessed. Skills are selected and presented in a context that enables learners to perform authentic tasks.

Generic information-skills lists are best used when they are customised, through selecting, categorising and labelling target skills, to meet academic needs and accommodate grade levels, using the facilities and resources available. Figure 2 presents five categories of information skills from an integrated library/information technology programme for middle schoolers. It illustrates how the categorisation of skills can be used as touchstones to identify the specific skills needed in the project work, giving the teacher and librarian the flexibility to design projects that serve the academic curriculum as well as the information literacy agenda of the library programme.

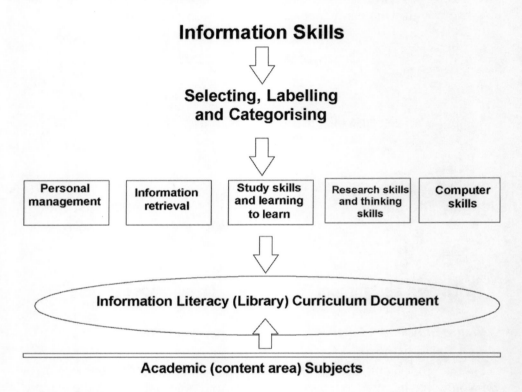

Figure 2: Customising an information skills list.

These categories, as well as the skills that are selected to appear in an information literacy curriculum document, structure the library instruction programme and present opportunities for interaction between the classroom and the library. Resources and facilities may limit the scope of categories of information skills that can be included in project work (*ie* computer skills are tool-based). However, thinking skills that provide depth and are related to the subject area, or academic context, in which information skills are embedded, are not tool-based and should not be excluded. All library programmes can be highly integrated and project-based. Librarians can ensure that all learners have opportunities to practice seminal information skills.

What this book does

No longer can the librarian limit her repertoire of teaching to lists of skills dictated by a curriculum document conceived in isolation. Information skills must emerge from the academic areas in which they are embedded. This book presents projects that artfully blend the information literacy agenda of the librarian with the agenda of the classroom teacher. Team teaching, interdisciplinary planning and teaching, integration of technology in teaching, and authentic, or performance-based learning and assessment, are comfortable partners to resource-based project work that highlights problem-solving, inquiry learning and critical thinking.

In these projects students assume the persona of a child living in their town during the Middle Ages and keep a diary that chronicles a day at the market place, or the adventures of becoming an apprentice to the village blacksmith. The Black Plague and a visit from the Lord of the Manor are seen through the eyes of a child. Students become Cultural Consultants and counsel families moving to the Middle East. Their own experiences as global nomads enable them to personalise the assignment and project their own experiences into it. Students investigate the relationship between smoking and health as they collect evidence from sources that survey real people as well as sifting through information sources, both print and electronic, to produce a brochure. Students become secret agents sent by their governments to explore historical, geographical and economic data about several European countries. Their reports are submitted to headquarters with recommendations for investment and development. Students become real researchers who generate their own data through interviews and surveys to explore anorexia, or learning disabilities, or child abuse. Often their research questions are connected to their own life experiences so that their engagement with the topics is more than an academic exercise aimed at a grade – they really want to know how to help a brother with a learning disability or a sister with anorexia. Students become designers as they weave a tapestry, create a computer program, plan and cook an Asian meal or construct a model of a Korean temple, choreograph a dance or perform an original play, or write and implement a program in bike safety for children.

The projects assembled in this book relate to a cross-section of academic subjects and a variety of grade levels, from third to twelfth. Most projects fall into middle level, from 5th to 9th grades, making adaptation of the units manageable for lower and upper grades. While the projects described are complete, their features can be used to modify projects already in place in your school. Technology is used in some projects and all projects are resource-based. These projects are the grist in the curriculum process; from them the information literacy skills that are considered most essential for academic success can be culled and incorporated in a curriculum that 'documents' what the library programme does to foster information literacy.

The **Reflections** section of each chapter identifies teaching concepts and issues in the context of the teacher-librarian collaboration. It highlights the role of the librarian as a reflective practitioner and the use of action research to involve students and teachers in critiquing project design and implementation. It addresses issues of performance-based authentic assessment measures and their place in the library programme. Each chapter contains a **Project Description** that is amplified by **Support Materials** that enable the reader to replicate the project. **Evaluation of Student Achievement** contains authentic assessment tools such as rubrics and journals, and the possibilities for connecting information literacy portfolios with project work. **Recommended Web Sites** are selected for their relevance to the projects. Exemplars of student work and full-text articles related to issues addressed in the Reflections have been placed on the ECIS web site.

The **Information Literacy Focus** in the head note of each chapter identifies skills that are central to the teaching and assessment of the unit. Projects cover a range of information literacy skills from location of materials to in-depth analysis of information and data. **Grade Level**, also indicated in the head note, denotes a range of grades for which the project, as written, is appropriate. All the skills covered are applicable, with editing for age-appropriateness, to all grade levels.

Information Literacy in Action is a collection of projects conceived by teachers and were intended to meet real needs, such as covering the curriculum, in the real world of every-day teaching. Each project has been piloted, implemented, revised and re-visited many times. As the world outside the classroom raced on to the Information Highway and online resources, and pedagogy translated constructivist ideas about learning to performance-based authentic learning and assessment, these projects survived dissection and, in some cases, extensive surgery. It is a tribute to the vision and reflective practice of the teachers whose work is represented here that their ideas are the backbone of several information literacy programmes in classrooms and libraries of international schools throughout Europe.

Special acknowledgement is due to the following educators:

Steve Casteldine, Istanbul International Community School
Bob Conley, American School in London
John Cordwell, Frankfurt International School
Sue Corlett, Frankfurt International School
Christian Decker, American School in The Hague
Andrew MacDonald, Frankfurt International School
Stephanie Vernon, International School of Monaco
Nicole Whelan, American School in The Hague
Ali Wills, International School of Monaco
Shona Wright, Geneva International School

The author would like to thank ECIS for encouragement and support in this endeavour.

Chapter One

Learning the Language of the Library

Activity One:	Decoding Deweyville
Level:	Grades 3-8
Interdisciplinary Action:	Geography, art, mathematics, modern languages
Information Literacy Focus:	Locating and retrieving information
Project Designer:	Carol Gordon

Project description

Do your students speak the language of Melville Dewey? Are they able to travel through the library, retrieving materials independently? This unit will take them to the town of Deweyville, a geographic metaphor for the Dewey Decimal System that offers opportunities to look at library organisation from spatial and cultural points of view. Learning activities link location skills with classroom lessons on community and geography, offering opportunities for students to build a multicultural community. Students collaborate to build the town, which can take the form of a map, a mural or a model. Construction of Deweyville could be a class project or a grade level activity.

Located off the Information Highway, Deweyville has only ten streets, an island, and a mountain. These features correspond to the library's main divisions: non-fiction, fiction and biography. Whether Deweyville is a small town or a booming metropolis (its population is the number of materials in your library), it contains countless treasures! Names of streets, such as 'Church Street' and 'Mr Fix-it Expressway,' help students remember Dewey categories. Deweyville addresses correspond to call numbers that mark the location of library materials. Books, authors, or references to a cultural context (eg the teachers in your school, words in the Spanish language, or historical figures) become members of the Deweyville community. Students use their imagination to adapt, customise and elaborate on ways to build the town as they explore concepts of family and community in a multi-cultural context. Collaboration with a geography teacher adds dimensions of site and situation for older students.

The streets off Deweyville Drive house non-fiction Dewey subjects. Fantasy Island, the land of fiction, and Biography Bluff are situated on the outskirts of Deweyville.

The support materials in this chapter include a map of Deweyville and suggestions for bringing the town to life with buildings, people, businesses and a landmark to its founder, Melville Dewey.

Enjoy your stay in Deweyville!

Support materials (p23-27)

A. How did Dewey Invent the System?
B. Map of Deweyville
C. Drawing a Blueprint for Deweyville
D. Deweyville Directory
E. Planning the Dewey Memorial

Activity Two:	Deweyville in Outer Space
Level:	Grades 6-9
Interdisciplinary Action:	Mathematics, science
Information Literacy Focus:	Location and retrieval of library materials
Project Designer:	Carol Gordon

Project description

Deweyville in Outer Space examines classification and sequencing. It explores the mathematical concepts of decimal place and notation, as well as the concept of infinity. It can also be cognitively linked to classification in science through labelling and categorising. This unit is timely for 6th graders, when they are introduced to decimals, and can be adapted for older students.

Support materials A and B are helpful for explaining the organisational structure of the Dewey system and the meaning of the decimal. Using the 900 category presents a concrete example of Dewey's system as he applied it to categorise countries of the world. Discussion of the 900 numbers will help students to understand how to build a decimal number, going from general to specific. Students will enjoy trying to build a Dewey number for the town or city and country from which they come. The problem, presented in Support Material A, engages students in the hypothetical situation of extending the system beyond the number 999 in order to create a library on a planet in our solar system other than Earth. Assuming the role of librarian, each student's task is to design a set of numbers beginning with 999, which is reserved for extraterrestrial worlds in the Dewey schedule. (Students usually want to see the last page of the Dewey schedules to verify this.) Their plans must use decimals added to 999 that can be used to classify books about the history of their planet.

The Science teacher will welcome the opportunity for an astronomy lesson to help students identify the planets, their distance from the sun, and the concept of other solar systems and galaxies.

The Mathematics teacher will appreciate this unit at the end of an introductory unit on decimals or as an opportunity to review decimals.

Key characteristics of the Dewey system can be elicited from students using the following questions:

How many whole digits does every number in the Dewey Decimal System have?

What is the smallest whole number? How is it written?

What is the largest whole number? How is it written?

Support materials (p28-31)

A. How Did Dewey Divide the World?
B. What About the Decimal?
C. What Comes After 999?
D. One Solution

Activity Three:	Reading the library shelves
Level:	Grades 6-8
Interdisciplinary Action:	Mathematics
Information Literacy Focus:	Location and retrieval of library materials; personal management skills
Project Designers:	Ellen Alquist, Carol Gordon

Project description

Students work in groups of three to read the library shelves to which they are assigned in order to identify those books that are misshelved. Since this activity requires close supervision, it is helpful to stagger student groups over a long enough period of time so that an adult can help each group of three students. Parent or high school volunteers may be recruited to help. Each student in the group is responsible for one section of a bookcase. **When a misshelved book is found it is moved to its proper location and turned on its side.** Students record how many books they have found out of order (Refer to the worksheet below.) An adult checks the work of each student to ensure that the books have been moved to their proper places on the shelves. Students write a report to the librarian using the guidelines listed in Support Material A.

Support materials (p32)

    A.   Student's Report
    B.   The Librarian's Report

Activity Four	Concentration
Level:	Grades 2-8
Interdisciplinary Action:	Language arts, ESL
Information Literacy Focus:	Building a library vocabulary
Project Designer:	Carol Gordon

Project description

Students play the *Concentration* game in groups of four. Each group receives a pack of cards. (Each pack can be colour-coded using markers or index cards for easy collation of the cards at the end of the lesson.) There is a card for each library word or term and for each definition. Students take turns turning over two cards. The object of the game is to match each card with its definition. When a match is made the student keeps the pair of cards and gets another turn. The student with the greatest number of pairs at the end of the game is the winner.

This activity is very helpful for ESL students whose teachers may keep several sets of *Concentration* cards in their classrooms. English teachers may include the library vocabulary in their lessons.

It is helpful to include vocabulary work in library orientation, especially for ESL students. Signs that correspond to the terminology on the playing cards can be posted on library walls as markers for orientation activities.

Signage in the library is an important part of an orientation program. Posters that explain each of the major sections of the library and the key words featured in the game of *Concentration* are important visuals that can be linked to a student search for answers to location questions about the library. Maintaining the signage and posters throughout the year is important for new students who arrive continuously throughout the school year as well as for ESL students.

Support materials (p33-34)

Building a library vocabulary

Evaluation of Student Achievement

Should we evaluate all information literacy topics that we teach? It is said that what is assessed is what gets taught and, more importantly, what gets learned. While we may not test everything, we need to assess or evaluate student progress in a consistent and reliable way.

Quizzes, oral or written, are reliable markers for student retention of the ten Dewey categories. Whenever possible, it is optimal to integrate the assessment with a content area. If collaborating with an art teacher to build Deweyville, for example, criteria can be established which address both the aesthetics of Deweyville and student application of the Dewey categories. If students produce individual maps of Deweyville they can be filed in their Information Literacy portfolios, or their art portfolios, accompanied by a written description of their work and response to the assigned task.

The Deweyville project is well suited to cross-grade activities. Fourth graders could build a model of Deweyville as a visual aid to teach the concepts of the Dewey Decimal System to second or third graders. A student-generated rubric is a good exercise for older elementary students. It guides their thinking toward standards that address the organisational elements of the Dewey Decimal System.

Quizzes and other conventional forms of testing do not assess whether students grasp the concepts of information handling. Evaluating a student's fluency in library language requires an ongoing form of assessment. A problem-solving exercise, such as the one described in *Dewey in Outer Space* can be evaluated by peer review as students share their solutions. Each group writes a short response at the end of the presentations, indicating the strengths and weaknesses of their solutions. These responses can be in the form of a written paragraph, or a graphic organisor (concept map, web drawing) that illustrates thought processes. The evaluation is substantive, rather than quantitative and does not require a grade.

Assessing fluency in the language of the library is best done through a medium that requires students to speak and write the language. Since information literacy skills are cumulative, portfolios that travel with students from grade to grade are ideal. Within this portfolio are reflective entries which document the student's self-evaluations as they apply the language of information handling.

While everything does not have to be tested, students should have frequent and ongoing opportunities to self-assess and to receive feedback from their teachers, librarians and classmates. Developing self-awareness of their progress in information literacy will prepare students to become their own best critics.

Reflection

Do we really need to teach the Dewey Decimal System?

A critical piece of information literacy is the ability to find information. Location skills are often taught in the context of student assignments, which helps meet immediate information needs but does not allow time for students to decipher the logic of the Dewey Decimal System. The system is more than a code for shelving library materials. It is a knowledge management system that classifies all that we know and can learn in ten categories with, theoretically, an infinite number of sub-divisions. Understanding its structure helps students to understand how we organise and categorise knowledge as well as the logic and mechanisms of information retrieval systems.

The confusion that the Internet has brought to information retrieval issues is rooted in the misconception that we can find anything we need on the net. This fallacy resides not in the possibility that everything might not be on the Internet, but in the assumption that every Internet site is organised – that it is a library, *ie*, a knowledge management system that makes it possible to retrieve information by searching for it. A prerequisite for successful search and retrieval is knowledge of the structure of the system that delivers retrieval information. Traditional principles of organisation such as title, author, and subject are the mainstay of a library catalogue, providing searchable fields. This catalogue assumes that the materials themselves have been organised so that they can be retrieved. As information specialists tackle the problem of cataloguing in cyberspace there is growing consensus that there will be several organisational systems to accommodate the diversity of information in terms of format and content, the amount of digitalised information, and the instability and constantly changing nature of the information. The constructs that become the principles of organisation of digitalised information will relate to the systems that organise information. Students who have achieved an understanding of one system will be better prepared to cope with more complex infrastructures in a digital world.

Support Materials
for Chapter One

Activity 1:   Decoding Deweyville
Information Literacy Focus: Locating and retrieving
                                     information

A. How did Dewey invent the system?

The problem

Dewey observed that libraries arranged books in fixed places: the same book was always in the same place on the same shelf all the time. When a borrowed book was returned it went back to the exact same place on the shelf. The first books acquired by the library were placed on the first shelf of the first bookcase and the most recently acquired book on the last shelf of the last bookcase. The book stayed in its assigned place forever. For example, if you wanted to find a book on sharks it would always be in the fourth bookcase, second section, third shelf, at the end of the row.

> What is wrong with this arrangement?
> What problems would arise when new books are added to the library collection?
> What are other ways to arrange books?
> What is the best way to arrange library materials so that they are easy to find regardless of which library you visit?

Hint

Melville Dewey asked himself, "Why not classify a book once and for all? Why not give a book an address (notation) that is true from shelf to shelf, from range to range, and from building to building?"

Day and night Dewey thought about the problem. Then, as the story goes, one morning in May 1873, an idea came to him when he was sitting in the Amherst Chapel.

"After months of study, one Sunday during a long sermon by Pres. Stearns, while I lookt stedfastly at him without hearing a word, my mind absorbed in the vital problem, the solution flasht over me so that I jumpt in my seat and came very near shouting 'Eureka'! It was to get absolute simplicity by using the simplest known symbols..."

The solution

Dewey decided to use numbers as symbols for the subjects of library books.

B. Map of Deweyville

Population:_____

Dewey Drive
300-399

Information
Highway
→

Odds and Ends
Boulevard
001 - 199

Science Street
500 - 599

Thinking Thruway
100 - 199

Mr Fix-It
Expressway
600 - 699

Worship Way
200 - 299

Fun Freeway
700 - 799

Community Court
300 - 399

Poems and Plays
Parkway
800 - 899

Words Way
400 - 499

History Highway
900 - 999

Fantasy Island FIC SC

Biography Bluff BIO 920

C. Drawing a blueprint for Deweyville

Listed below is a guide to the streets of Deweyville that defines the categories of the Dewey Decimal System.

Address	Street Name	Street Subject
001-099	Odds and Ends Avenue	Information that does not fit into the other nine categories. Examples: Encyclopaedias, books about libraries, journalism.
100-199	Thinking Thruway	Information about the mind and things that cannot be explained. Example: The Loch Ness Monster
200-299	Worship Way	Information about religion. Examples: The Bible; The Koran
300-399	Community Court	Information about living together in a society. Example: Rules and regulations (laws)
400-499	Words Way	Information about languages. Example: Dictionaries
500-599	Science Street	Information about Math and Science. Examples: Counting books; Books about sharks
600-699	Mr Fix-It Expressway	Information about fixing, making and creating things. Examples: Farming, medicine
700-799	Fun Freeway	Information about sports, music, art and recreation. Examples: How to play chess; The story of the *Nutcracker* ballet; The art of Walt Disney; Rules of cricket
800-899	Plays and Poems Parkway	Poems and plays Examples: *A Light in the Attic*; *Peter Pan-The Musical*
900-999	History Highway	Information about history and geography. Examples: Atlases, travel guides, books about countries

D. Deweyville Directory

What makes a community? The items listed in the Directory will help students to identify the elements of a town while learning the Dewey categories.

001-099	Library 024.4 Deweyville University 027.7 Deweyville Museum 069
100-199	Loch Ness Monster 133.3 Palm Reading 133.6
200-299	Lutheran Church 284.1 Synagogue 296 Church of Latter-Day Hindu Temple 294.5 Saints 289.3 Islamic Mosque 297
300-399	Deweyville Bank 332.1 Police Department 363.2 Courthouse 347 Electric Company 363.32 Firehouse 352.3 07 Melville Dewey Elementary Storybook Village 398 School 372.24
400-499	Modern Language Bookstore 400 Russian Dictionary Section 491.7 English Dictionary section 420 Japanese Dictionary Section 495.6 French Dictionary section 440 Korean Dictionary Section 495.7 Spanish Dictionary section 460 Bantu Dictionary Section 496.39
500-599	Planetarium 519 Deweyville Zoo 570 Electric Company 537 Botanical Gardens 580
600-699	Red Cross 610.734 Train Station 625.1 Pharmacy 615.1 Highway Department 625.7 Deweyville Hospital 616 Airport 629.136 Dr Floss 617.6 Supermarket 641
700-799	Halloween Costume Shoppe 746.92 Deweyville Photography 770 The Music Store 780 Deweyville Circus 791.3 Golf Course 796.35264
800-899	International Bookstore 800 French books section 840 Chinese books section 895.1 South American books section 898
900-999	Travel Agency 910 Egyptian Embassy 962 Deweyville Hall of Fame 920 Australian Embassy 994 British Embassy 945

E. Planning the Dewey Memorial

Melville Louis Kossuth Dewey
Founder of Deweyville
(aka: Melvil Dui, Melvil Dewey)

1851-1931

1851	Born in Adams Center, New York on December 10th (The 10th day of the 10th month, according to the early Roman republican calendar).
1868	Taught school.
1876	Published the Dewey Decimal classification system. Founded Library Bureau in Boston, Massachusetts... 'for the definite purpose of furnishing libraries with equipment and supplies of unvarying correctness and reliability.' Organised the first conference for librarians in Philadelphia at which the American Library Association (ALA) was born.
1886	Founded the Spelling Reform Association. Worked for 60 years to make spelling simpler. He liked to write words the way they sounded (*eg* taut, giv, vilaj, plenti, bizness, nobodi, wud, tym, skool, studid, ges, muni, walkt, hav). He even invented new letters.
1890	Elected President of ALA. Elected again in 1892.
1897	Served as the official delegate of the US Government to the International Library Conference in London.
1931	Died on December 26th.

Where in Deweyville would you build the memorial to Melville Dewey?

Activity 2:   Deweyville in Outer Space

Information Literacy Focus: Location and retrieval of
                                      library materials

A. How did Dewey divide the world?

Use examples from the 900s, like the ones below, to illustrate the hierarchy and structure of whole numbers in the Dewey Decimal System.

900	History, Geography
920	Biography
930	History of Ancient Worlds
940	History of Europe
943	History of Germany
950	History of Asia
960	History of Africa
970	History of North America
971	History of Canada
972	History of Middle America
973	History of USA
970	History of North America
980	History of South America
990	History of Other Parts
993	New Zealand
994	Australia
995	Melanesia/New Guinea
996	Polynesia/Southwest Pacific
997	Atlantic Ocean Islands
998	Arctic and Antarctica
999	Extraterrestrial Worlds

B. What about the decimal?

This chart helps students to understand how a Dewey Decimal number is constructed as they observe the function of the decimal.

9 0 0	History, Geography
9 7 0	North America
9 7 1	Canada
9 7 2	Middle America
9 7 3	Northeastern U.S.A.
9 7 4	Massachusetts
9 7 4. 4	Barnstable County
9 7 4. 4 9	Town of Barnstable

C. What comes after 999?

The problem posed in this unit challenges students to extend the Dewey Decimal Classification beyond the digit 999. Students can work in teams; each team presents a solution using the overhead projector or chalkboard. Students assess each other's solutions. The clues listed below can be given to students if they are having difficulty with the solution.

The problem

Choose a planet and pretend it has been colonised and that you have moved there. You are the librarian and your job is to catalogue the books in the main library that chronicle the history of your new planet. Devise a decimal system that you can use to catalogue a book about the HISTORY of the capital city of your planet. Your system should permit inclusion of all the planets that travel around the Earth's sun as well as the possibility of other galaxies.

Helpful hints

1. Draw a picture of our universe including the sun, moon, and planets. Use the table below to record the numbers you would use in your solution.

HUNDREDS	TENS	ONES	Decimal Point	TENTHS	HUNDREDS
9					
9					
9					
9					
9					
9					
9					
9					
9					
9					
9					
9					
9					

2. If every Dewey Decimal whole number has three digits, what is the largest whole number? What is the smallest whole number? (How would we write it so it has three digits?)
3. If the highest whole number is 999, how can we have a larger number that is less than 1,000?
4. If every hundred's place indicates a new category, how many Dewey categories are there? What happens to a subject as we move to the right of the decimal point?

D. One solution

999	Extraterrestrial worlds
999.1	Earth's moon
999.2	Planets of solar system
999.21	Mercury
999.22	Venus
999.23	Mars + 2 satellites
999.24	Asteroids (Planetoids)
999.25	Jupiter + 12 satellites
999.26	Saturn + 10 satellites
999.27	Uranus + 5 satellites
999.28	Neptune + 2 satellites
999.29	Pluto + transplutonian planets
999.3	Meteoroids and comets
999.4	Sun

Activity 3:   Reading the library shelves
Information Literacy Focus: Location and retrieval of
                                     library materials; personal
                                     management skills

A. Student's report

Name _____

Date _____

Time Started _____

Time finished _____

Total number of minutes spent reading the shelves _____

Number of books 'read' on your shelves _____

Number of books found out of Dewey Decimal order _____

Please give your report to the librarian _____

B. The Librarian's report

A follow-up report from the librarian, like the one shown below, is sent to each class which participated in reading the shelves. The teacher shares it with her students.

Dear Students

Thank you for helping to read the library shelves. As you can see, it is a big job! It is also an important job because if a book is out of order on the shelves it may as well be lost. Would you look for a book in the wrong place? How much time do you think [name of teacher] 6th grade class spent reading the shelves? **Answer: 13 hours and 36 minutes**.

How many book labels do you think the 6th graders read? **Answer: 6,490** What do you estimate was the average number of spine labels read by a 6th grader? (There were 95 students reading the shelves.) **Answer: 68.3 spine labels.**

How many books do you estimate we have in the library? **Answer: 26,000.** How long do you estimate it would take 95 Grade 6 students to read the spine labels for every book in the library? **Answer: 54 hours and 24 minutes.**

I think you will agree that if people are not careful the library staff could spend most of their time putting books in the right places instead of helping people!

[name of teacher] and I would like to thank you for helping us in the library by saving us 13 hours and 36 minutes of work by taking care of the library's 6490 books!

[name of librarian]

Activity 4:   Concentration

Information Literacy Focus: Building a library vocabulary

Each library word or term and each definition is recorded on separate cards.

Spine
> The part of the book that connects the front and back cover and contains the book's call number.

Fiction (novel)
> A book whose story is based on the author's imagination.

Non-fiction
> A book that includes information, facts and actual events.

Dewey Decimal number
> The numbers on the spine of a book that indicate where the book belongs on the library shelves.

Call number
> The Dewey number and letters (*eg*, author's last name) on the spine of a book that indicate where the book is shelved.

Library catalogue
> The index to library materials that tells you where to find them on the shelves.

Reference
> Books that are used for research that cannot be checked out of the library, or that are checked out for overnight only.

Microfiche
> Film, in the form of cards, that contains photographs of newspaper or magazine pages that have been reduced in size and can be read using a machine called a microfiche reader.

Index
> An alphabetical list of subjects or topics (sometimes found at the end of a book) that contains information to help you locate information or materials.

Readers' Guide to Periodical Literature
> The index for magazines.

Electronic resources
> Information that has been digitalised so that you can read it on a computer.

Story collections (SC)
> Books that contain short stories that are fiction.

Biography
A book about the life of a person.

Collected biographies
A book about the lives of several people.

Periodical
Magazine or newspaper.

Circulation desk
The place you go to check out library materials.

Recommended web sites

Expanded Introduction to the Dewey Decimal Classification – includes detailed outline of the Dewey Decimal System.
http://www.oclc.org/oclc/fp/about

Let's Do Dewey – includes explanations and activities for children to practise location skills.
http://www.mtsu.edu/~vvesper/dewey.html

Dewey Screen Savers and Wallpaper – download a screen saver to your library computers that displays the ten Dewey categories.
http://www.oclc.org/oclc/fp/products/#screensaver

Chapter Two

Taking Note of History

Activity:	Back to the Middle Ages
Level:	Grades 4-7
Interdisciplinary Action:	Social studies/humanities; English/language arts
Information Literacy Focus:	Evaluating information and sources
Project Designer:	Bob Conley, American Schoolin London

Project description

Students travel back in time to create and assume a 15th century identity for themselves. Their task is to write a historically accurate five-day illustrated diary about life as the son of a serf or the daughter of a merchant living in Oberursel, Germany. The diary is written from the point of view of an 11- or 12-year-old. Students are randomly assigned their 'persona'. The diary chronicles five days in the life of a medieval family. *LBMS – The Middle Ages*, a web site, created by 7th grade students to teach about life in the Middle Ages, is a perfect lead-in for the unit. It includes illustrated articles, student artwork, and *Life as a...* stories. Students would benefit from viewing this site prior to library research at
http://schools.ci.burbank.ca.us/~luther/midages/beginhere.html

Student research takes place in the library for four days. Library books are placed on reserve so that library time can focus on note taking. The Student Packet features graphic organisers, which help students to select relevant information and organise it in note form. To prepare for writing, students develop a Personal Profile and Personal Time Line. The entries must include the date, historically correct information, and glossary terms provided in the Student Packet. Each day has a theme, as shown in the note taking sheets, or graphic organisers, in the Student Packet. The humanities/social studies teacher works with the English/language arts teacher to use the writing process (Plan, Compose, Revise, Edit, and Publish). The English teacher uses a bibliography of historical fiction found in the school library prepared by the librarian, to direct student reading to novels with medieval settings.

What was it really like to live in the Middle Ages? a video series in the Annenberg/CPB Multimedia Collection, inspired by programmes from *The Western Tradition*, contains well-illustrated information on daily life in the Middle Ages, including food, housing, clothing and occupations. This site offers a supplementary or alternative resource to text. It is also a good source for the planning and brainstorming phase of the writing process. Go to **http://www.learner.org/exhibits/middleages**

There are several web sites, listed at the end of this chapter, which are well-illustrated and written for children.

Students are instructed that their drawings should be appropriate for each day and illustrate something mentioned in the diary. Two of the following six Oberursel historical sites must appear in the drawings:

1. City wall
2. Urselbach
3. Market
4. St Ursela's Church
5. Rathaus/town gate
6. Witch's steps

A Bibliography Chart, which is a graphic organiser for recording sources used to gather information, also requires students to evaluate their sources. Students apply criteria, or standards, from the Rubric for a Good Book Source (*opposite*), which include: accuracy; authority; objectivity; coverage; usefulness. Students use these standards, with accompanying descriptors, to rate each source as 1 or 0. They place their rating in the last column of the Bibliography Chart (*see p56*). Along with the rating, students give an example of a good or poor quality relative to one of the standards for good sources. The rubric can be adapted to the information needs and grade level of the students. For example, a rubric for older students may not include 'illustrations' in the descriptor for 'Usefulness'. A science assignment may include 'Currency' as a standard. It is also important to vary the format of the source evaluated. Students should have opportunities in other assignments to apply rubrics to periodicals, electronic resources and web sites.

Bibliography Charts for various formats (*eg*, book, periodical, web site) should be provided in the Student Packet and a supply of these charts made available in the library. Each entry (*eg* title, author, URL or web address) should appear in the same order as the formal citation, whether the style sheet used is APA, MLA, or Turabian. The librarian can provide leadership by getting consensus among faculty so that one method of citation is

Rubric for a Good Book Source

RATING	ACCURACY	AUTHORITY	OBJECTIVITY	COVERAGE	USEFULNESS
1	• has a bibliography of sources • contains correct facts all the time • documents or cites facts with footnotes or endnotes	• authors(s) or editor(s) are qualified by their education or experience to write on the topic • copyright is clearly stated on the title page	• goals or aims of the author(s) are clearly stated • facts, rather than opinion, support conclusions	• there is enough information on the topic • chapters cover important topics	• there is a table of contents • chapter headings help you choose which parts of the book to read • the index leads you to relevant information • there are illustrations • the reading level and presentation of the book was appropriate for you
0	• does not have a bibliography of sources • contains incorrect facts • does not document or cite facts with footnotes or endnotes	• there is no information about the author(s) or editor(s) • copyright is not given	• goals or aims of the author(s) or editor(s) are not clearly stated • opinion, rather than facts, support conclusions	• there is not enough information on the topic • chapters do not cover the time period or geographical location that you expected from the title or chapter headings	• there is no table of contents • chapter headings are not helpful for choosing which parts of the book to read • there is no index • there are no illustrations • the reading level was too low or too high for you

adopted school-wide. The Bibliography Chart is a good introduction to citation and prepares students for formal citation in high school. It is also a hedge against plagiarism and offers a good opportunity for the librarian to stress the importance of respecting intellectual property and acknowledging sources of information.

Students create an artefact that represents their 15th century lives (*eg* tool, toy, household item.) The artefact should be as realistic as possible regarding size, details, composition and appropriateness to the medieval social status of its maker. A short paragraph accompanies the artefact explaining how it was made, its use, and its significance. Artefacts are displayed in a *Medieval Museum* exhibit that is visited by other students and parents.

Interim deadlines are set for:
1. Personal Profile and Personal Time Line;
2. First drafts of Day One, Days Two and Three, Days Four and Five;
3. Two revisions of the five days completed;
4. Two edits of the five days completed;
5. Completely assembled research packet (see Support Materials);
6. Completed diary;
7. Artefact accompanied by a descriptive paragraph.

The teacher introduces the Student Packet, included in the Support Materials section of this chapter, prior to library sessions that are used for note taking. The emphasis is on content and using the graphic organisers for note taking, the final outcomes, or projects required and the assessment rubric. The librarian uses the packet for a short introduction to the resources which, in this case, are placed on a reserve cart. Instructions for the use of the Bibliography Chart include standards for evaluating book sources, which is also covered in class prior to research in the library.

The rubric used to assess students' diaries draws from the English department's rubric for writing (*ie*, standards for Vocabulary/Style and Mechanics). The ratings of 4-1 can correspond to A, B, C and D or number grades (*see page 40-41*).

Support materials (p47-58)

A. Middle Ages Glossary
B. Personal Profile: Who Am I?
C. Time Lines
D. Note Taking Sheet Day One: Description of My Family and Me
E. Note Taking Sheet Day Two: Description of My Home
F. Note taking Sheet Day Three: Description of My Father's/Mother's Job
G. Note taking Sheet Day Four: Description of My Town
H. Note taking Sheet Day Five: Choice of Events to describe
I. Bibliography Chart for Books

Evaluation of Student Achievement

The evaluation of this project should include product (the diary) and process (the Student Packet). Each should be given a weight of 50% of the grade to highlight the importance of the information literacy focus, note taking, and other elements of the process.

A. Writing project rubric for Middle Ages diary
See page 42

B. Point system for Student Packet

The Student Packet documents process and is a good assessment for the information literacy focus of this unit, *ie*, note taking. Process, as well as product (which is assessed in this unit by a rubric) should be assessed and given equal weight for a final grade. A point system is one way the Student Packet can be graded.

5 points	Personal Profile
10 points	Personal Time Line
25 points	Note Taking Pages (5 points for each page)
10 points	Bibliography Chart

Total 50 points

C. Rating the artefact

This part of the learning task presents an opportunity for students to generate standards for a good artefact. Class discussion and group work will help students come to a consensus about the standards. An exemplar of a good artefact is a helpful aid for students to progress from the object they will create to descriptors. Students can apply their rubrics during the exhibit of artefacts. Their ratings can then be compared with the ratings given by the teacher.

Reflection
The place of evaluation in Information Literacy

Students are faced with exercising their evaluation skills when they choose a source of information and when they select information from the source. They are also self-evaluating continuously in terms of their progress in getting through the assignment. Their participation in rating their work offers another opportunity for evaluating the products they create. Note taking, of all the evaluative research activities consumes the most time and is probably the most frustrating of skills to teach and learn. Here is a typical scenario.

Ms Martinez felt she had prepared her 7th grade Humanities class for a research assignment. She engaged students in lessons about economic indicators as they relate to developed and developing countries. She had collaborated with the librarian, using a process approach to teach relevant research skills. She had prepared an extensive vocabulary list to help the students' search for library materials. She had emphasised that students paraphrase and avoid copying 'word for word.' Her students entered the library, paragons of good behaviour, in single file and in silence. Seated in a remote corner they listened carefully to instructions, their furrowed brows conveying deep concentration. They approached the books that had been placed on reserve with caution as the librarian extolled the virtues of cumulative indexes and cross-references. Released from this instructional spell, they poked through the collection as if looking for a friendly face in a hostile crowd. Returning to their seats, they began to read, carefully placing their 'shopping list' notes on the appropriate note-taking sheets in their packets. As they moved from the first resource book to others, each trip to the library shelves became more circuitous, as if the effort of weaving a tortuous path would ensure a just reward. Movements became increasingly quick and awkward as the first encyclopaedic volume hit the floor with a resounding thud. It was as though the shot had been fired and the race had begun. Traffic patterns became more direct as students scurried from desks to library shelves and back again, leaving books in chaos with no regard for Melville Dewey and his decimal points. The scene had swung into a fast-forward mode. Gestures grew more expansive: voices escalated in volume and pitch. Neat, legible notes degenerated to chicken scratch. Andrew, who had been making frequent trips to the dictionary, looked exhausted as he posed his question, "Ms Martinez, Ms Martinez, what's another word for 'for'?"
"Why," quizzed Ms Martinez, "do you need a synonym for a preposition?"
"Well, you told us not to copy word for word and to use our own words."
With horror she realised that Andrew had been translating the World Book Encyclopaedia, one painful word at a time. Meanwhile, Ann was frantically gathering geographical evidence of Ethiopia's status. She had conscientiously gone through her alphabetised glossary of words, finally reaching 'vegetation.'
"Mrs Gordon, Mrs Gordon," she screamed above the din that now filled the room, "is fish a vegetable?"

Students have difficulty transferring what they learn in class about skimming, using headings and subheadings in the text, looking for key words and making 'note cards.' Many strategies like these fail for novice researchers when note taking is taught as a mechanical activity, with not enough attention to structuring the complex thought processes, (ie the evaluation, selection and ordering of information) that direct the activity of note taking. The scenario described above makes it clear that taking notes is a complex intellectual

Writing project rubric for Middle Ages diary

	HISTORICAL INFORMATION	EMPATHY	DEVELOPMENT	VOCABULARY/STYLE
4	• all information is historically correct • historical information blends in very well • all information reflects the values of the time • all illustrations are historically correct	• the recreated situation is very realistic • clear evidence the writer understands the living conditions and life style of the time	• topic developed very well and reflects original thinking • evidence that the writer is aware of the audience • writing is always focused and on the topic	• required number of glossary terms used • all terms are used in an appropriate and clever way • the writing is descriptive, vivid, and fluent throughout
3	• nearly all information is historically correct • historical information blends in well • most information reflects the values of the time • most illustrations are historically correct	• the recreated situation is usually realistic • fairly clear evidence the writer understands the living conditions and life style of the time	• topic developed quite well and reflects some original thinking • evidence that the writer is usually aware of the audience • writing is usually focused and on the topic	• required number of glossary terms used • most terms are used in an appropriate and clever way • the writing is usually descriptive, vivid, and fluent
2	• some information is historically correct • historical information blends • some information reflects the values of the time • some illustrations are historically correct	• the recreated situation is sometimes realistic • sometimes clear evidence the writer understands the living conditions and life style of the time	• topic somewhat developed; reflects some original thinking • the writer is some-times aware of the audience • writing is some-times focused and on the topic	• almost all of the required number of glossary terms used • some terms are used in an appropriate and clever way • the writing is some-times descriptive, vivid, and fluent
1	• little information is historically correct • historical information does not blend in well • little information reflects the values of the time • few illustrations are historically correct	• the recreated situation is not usually realistic • little or no evidence the writer understands the living conditions and life style of the time	• topic not well developed; reflects little original thinking • the writer is hardly ever aware of the audience • writing is not focused and on the topic	• few of the required number of glossary terms used • few terms are used in an appropriate and clever way • the writing is usually not descriptive, vivid, and fluent

	MECHANICS	FORMAT	ARTEFACT
4	• few or no spelling, punctuation, capitalisation or grammatical errors • paragraphing is correct	• the diary looks as original as possible • very neatly done • all days are dated	• great care was taken in construction to be neat and accurate • appropriate materials were used • historically accurate • looks and feels accurate
3	• few or no spelling, punctuation, capitalisation or grammatical errors • paragraphing is correct	• the diary looks quite original • fairly neatly done • all days are dated	• much care was taken in construction to be neat and accurate • usually appropriate materials were used • historically accurate • looks and feels quite accurate
2	• some spelling, punctuation, capitalisation or grammatical errors that do hinder under-standing • paragraphing fairly correct	• the diary does not look very original • fairly neatly done • most days are dated	• some care was taken in construction to be neat and accurate • some appropriate materials were used • contains historical inaccuracies • looks and feels fairly accurate
1	• many spelling, punctuation, capitalisation or grammatical errors that may interfere with understanding • paragraphing is mostly incorrect	• the diary does not look very original • not neatly done • most days are not dated	• little or no care was taken in construction to be neat and accurate • few appropriate materials were used • not historically accurate; does not look or feel historically accurate

activity strongly related to the information search, where discrimination between relevant and irrelevant material is critical. Teaching vocabulary, and even content knowledge, is not sufficient preparation for information searching and note-taking. Graphic organisers address thought processes and can be used for a variety of purposes. In *Back to the Middle Ages* the note taking sheets structure the collection of information. The time line helps students to sequence information.

A Bibliography Chart guides students in the organisation and documentation of sources and can also structure their evaluation of each sources using criteria previously established in class. Bibliography Charts can be adapted to any format and are useful in preparing students for formal citation. When students are using a variety of formats it is important that the Bibliography Charts are tailored to the idiosyncracies of each format. For example, a citation from the Internet would not include city of publication or publisher. Evaluative criteria will also vary with format: 'Authority' criteria may be more of a concern when downloading from the web than when using a book from the school library. Go the web sites listed at the end of this chapter for more information on evaluating web resources.

Graphic organisers can support other thinking skills, such as analysis, synthesis and evaluation, as shown by the examples that follow.

Graphic Organiser A: Collecting Information

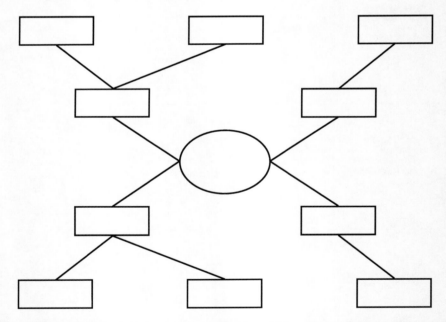

Graphic Organiser A is an example of webbing. It helps students to make connections and associations between and among information in a non-linear way. Mind mapping and concept mapping are variations of this organiser. See Recommended Web Sites for detailed information on these techniques.

Graphic Organiser B: Ordering information

The triangular graphic can be used as shown, or turned 180 degrees to order, sequence, or prioritise information. When students use their own notes in the selection process they have the opportunity to evaluate how effectively and efficiently they took notes. This organiser can also serve as a preliminary outline of subheadings that emerge from their notes.

Graphic Organiser C: Selecting and summarising information

The summary chart illustrates how a graphic organiser can be used to help students select information from their notes that support major points of analysis, such as cause and effect. When organisers are linked to specific methods of analysis student thinking is set in a framework that they can visualize.

The _____ Revolution was a unique historical event but shares common elements with the French Revolution.

Main Causes

_____ Revolution   French Revolution

_____   _____

_____   _____

Main Effects

_____ Revolution   French Revolution

_____   _____

_____   _____

Main Events

_____ Revolution   French Revolution

_____   _____

_____   _____

Graphic Organiser D: Analyzing information

An analytical chart illustrates how a graphic organiser can be designed to support analysis of facts. In this example students compared and contrasted the French Revolution, which was taught in class, with a revolution they researched. Students chose information from their notes to use as supporting evidence.

Your Revolution   French Revolution

How are they the same ?

How are they different ?

In addition to evaluating sources and information, students need opportunities to evaluate their own work and the work of their peers. Raising their awareness of standards and exercising their skills in applying standards help them to become good evaluators. See **Reflections**, Chapter 5 for more information about rubrics.

Support Materials
for Chapter Two

Activity: Back to the Middle Ages

Information Literacy Focus: Evaluating information and
                                              sources

A. Middle Ages glossary

Agriculture   farming the soil to produce crops and raising livestock.

Apprentice   a young person learning a craft from a master craftsman.

Cathedral   a large, important church.

Craftsman   a man who learned a skill and had his own shop, such as
a weaver, tanner or baker.

Crusades   a military expedition made by knights and kings to
recover the Holy Land from the Muslims. (11th - 13th
centuries.)

Dark Ages   the early Middle Ages (about 500 - 1000 AD).

Fair   a special market held once a year.

Feudalism   a system where landholders received protection in return
for work or military help.

Fief   a feudal estate.

Guild   a group of merchants or craftsmen.

Knight   a warrior, soldier, on horseback trained for battle for his
king or nobleman.

Market   a place where peasants brought their extra food to trade
with others.

Medieval   describes the Middle Ages.

Merchant   someone who buys or sells things for profit.

Monastery   a place where monks live and work.

Monk   a man who joined a religious group that works, studies
and prays in a monastery.

Noblemen   kings, dukes, or lords who were the landowners.

Occupation   a job.

Peasant   a serf.

Plague   a disease that spreads quickly and causes death. Also called Bubonic Plague and Black Death.

Serf   a poor person who lived on the lord's land and farmed it for him.

Squire   a knight's helper: a young man training to be a knight

Tithe   a part of a person's salary (one-tenth) that is given to the church or landowner as a tax.

Tournament   warlike games where knights practised their skills and attracted large crowds.

Trade   buying or selling things.

B. Personal profile: Who am I?

Name (21st century)_____

Name (Medieval) _____

Parents' occupation_____/_____
                                (father)   (mother)

Religion _____

Date of birth _____Age _____

Family members

Name	Age	Living or Dead?	Relationship	Job

C. Time lines

Historical time line

1400	1410	1420	1430	1438	1440	1444	1450	1457	1460	1470	1480	1484	1490	1492	1493	1500

1400	Rupprecht of Palantinate elected emperor Construction of St Ursela's church began
1410	Sigismund of Luxembourg elected emperor
1438	Albrecht of Hapsburg elected emperor
1440	Frederick III elected emperor
1444	Oberursel became a 'city' with population 940 1444 began building Rathaus (Town Hall)
1457	First book printed 1457-1500 177 Bibles printed in Latin
1480	Town wall and other fortifications built
1484	Oberursel's population reached 2,820
1492	Columbus sailed to America
1493	Maximilian I elected emperor

Personal time line

1400	1410	1420	1430	1438	1440	1444	1450	1457	1460	1470	1480	1484	1490	1492	1493	1500

D. Note-taking sheet

Day one
Description of my family and me

Date:

Food: What do I eat?	Clothes: What do I wear

Family: What is our family life like? (What is our daily routine? What do we do together?)

E. Note-taking sheet

Day two
Description of my home

Date:

Home: Where do I live? (What does my house look like?)
Inside
Outside (Size, Construction)
Surroundings

F. Note-taking sheet

Day three
Description of my father's/mother's job

Date:

What is my father's/mother's job?
(What are his/her responsibilities?)
What is his/her position in society? Rich? Poor?
What tools or instruments does he/she use?
Where does he/she work?)
Family member training/job
Work routines

G. Note-taking sheet

Day four
Description of my town

Date:

What are the buildings and important places in my town?	What do these buildings and places look like? Why are they important?
Historical background of the town: What are the important events and when did they happen?	Population information. Give the numbers and dates for every 50 years for the last 200 years.
What is the shape of the town?	What is the size of the town?

H. Note-taking sheet

Day five

Choose one of the following. Take 'shopping list' notes that will help you to describe the event.

Market day
A trip to Koenigstein or Frankfurt
An unexpected event
A special holiday or celebration
A trip to a monastery or fair
Remembering a family story or event from the past

Date:

Day Five

I. Bibliography chart for books

Fill out your chart for each book from which you take notes. You can find the information on the front and back of the book's title page. If the book has an editor(s) use the author column for the name(s). If you use a set of books (such as an encyclopaedia) write the volume number in the title column.

Rate each source in the last column of the chart. Use the Rubric for a Good Book Source, which can be found on page 37. Use a rating of 1 for a source that meets all the standards. A rating of 0 indicates the source does not meet the standard.

Author(s) or Editor(s)	Copy-right Date	Title (+ volume no.)	City of Publication	Publisher	Pages Used	How I rate this source
Howe, J	1995	Knights	New York	Orchard Books	1-10, 22, 35-40	1 good index

Recommended web sites

Graphic organisers

Graphic Organizers – displays several graphic organisers and explains the practical applications of each.
http://www.ncrel.org/sdrs/areas/issues/students/learning/lr1grorg.htm

Graphic Organizers Index – displays and explains types of graphic organisers, including webbing, concept mapping, matrix and flow chart.
http://www.graphic.org/goindex.html

Inspiration – a visual thinking and learning software programme. A trial programme can be downloaded from this site.
http://www.inspiration.com/

Time Liner —creates time lines. Includes download of a free demo.
http://www.tomsnyder.com/products/ProductList.asp?QryType= Subject&SubjectID=2

Write Design On-line Graphic Organizers – Defines five types of graphic organisers and the corresponding thought processes that they target.
http://www.writedesignonline.com/organizers/

Evaluating web resources

Evaluating Information Found on the World Wide Web
http://www.webliminal.com/search/search-web12.html

Evaluating Web Resources
http://www2.widener.edu/Wolfgram-Memorial-Library/ webevaluation/webeval.htm

The Good, The Bad and The Ugly, or Why It's a Good Idea to Evaluate Web Sources
http://lib.nmsu.edu/instruction/eval.html

ICYouSee: T is for Thinking
http://www.ithaca.edu/library/Training/hott.html

Internet Detective
http://sosig.ac.uk/desire/internet-detective.html

Thinking Critically About World Wide Web Resources
http://www.library.ucla.edu/libraries/college/instruct/web/critical.htm

Why We Need to Evaluate What We Find on the Internet
http://thorplus.lib.purdue.edu/~techman/eval.html

The Middle Ages

LBMS – The Middle Ages
http://schools.ci.burbank.ca.us/~luther/midages/beginhere.html

The Middle Ages in Europe – check out the link to Bubonic Plague
http://www.jordan.palo-alto.ca.us/students/connections/middle.html

What was it really like to live in the Middle Ages?
http://www.learner.org/exhibits/middleages/

Yahooligans! What it was really like to live in the Middle Ages
http://www.yahooligans.com/School_Bell/Social_Studies/History/Euro pe/Middle_Ages/

Chapter Three

Following the Path of Spiralling Resources

Activity:	Global Nomads Inc
Level:	Grades 6-8
Interdisciplinary Action:	Social studies/humanities; transition program; English, language arts; Information Technology
Information Literacy Focus:	Using print and electronic resources
Project Designers:	Christian Decker, Nicole Whelan, The American School in The Hague

Project description

This project is relevant to the lives of students enrolled in international schools who deal with transition on a regular basis. It is important for them to understand the benefits and challenges of living abroad and to call upon their personal experiences while working on Global Nomads Inc. Each student takes on the role of Cultural Consultant for a fictitious family moving to the Middle East. Authentic learning tasks help them to become experts in their project nations so they can help their clients to experience a smooth transition to their new host countries. Students become 'experts' as they produce:

1. Business letters to their client;
2. Memoranda and email messages informing the company CEO (the teacher) of works in progress;
3. A presentation and interview of a client who is pretending to move to the Middle East.

See **http://www.ash.nl/ms/grade7/gni/gni_homepage.html** for pictures and samples of student work.

Students selected their countries on the first day of the project. The first step in orienting students to the heart of the task was formulation of a research question. For example, *What information and advice would be useful for a family moving to Iran?* The broad aspects of the project were reviewed, including due dates and handouts. The following few days were used for research. A 'Scavenger Hunt' for information, using a multi-source approach, focused the search strategy. After a short orientation in the library to potential hardcover resources, such as reference materials and travel guides, students were introduced to the library's on-line resources. They were then given one period to find as much information as possible from the Scavenger Hunt list. The next day they were scheduled into the Computer Lab and given an orientation to various relevant CD-ROM titles (including *Encarta World Atlas; Encarta Encyclopedia*; and *Mindscape World Atlas*) and specific Internet sites pre-selected by the teacher (*CIA's Home Page for Kids* at **http://www.cia.gov/cia/ciakids/index.html** and the *Kid's Almanac* at **http://kids.infoplease.com/**). On the final day of research students were oriented to the use of Internet search engines and given two recommended search engines to try: *Ask Jeeves for Kids* at **http://www.ajkids.com/** and *Google* at **http://www.google.com/**. Any additional research was done outside class time. The following day students reflected on and discussed the process of research, particularly with regard to selection of sources, considering which sources were faster, more timely, and had the most reliable information.

Students examined the format of an official memorandum sent to them by their teacher/CEO of Global Nomads Inc. They wrote a memo to the CEO regarding contract work and preparations prior to meeting with their client and their families.

Various guest speakers were invited to speak with students about Middle Eastern countries. They delivered information focusing on culture, religion, tourism, climate, vegetation and facts that gave students insights about moving and living in selected countries. Members of the school community served as guest speakers.

A Cultural Consultant was invited to facilitate a workshop with students. She explained her job and how she helps families adjust to their new host countries. She organised a game to heighten students' awareness of cultural differences. Students were placed in five different groups. They were given a set of rules to play a card game and then asked to discard the rules. Students were not aware that each group had a different set of rules. They regrouped in a jigsaw activity and were asked to continue playing the card game without speaking to any members of their new group. They had to communicate through gestures and expressions. Some became frustrated when they realised that new members were playing by different rules! A discussion about cultural differences followed. Students expressed how they felt when they thought the game should have been played 'their' way.

They compared this game to past experiences they had had living abroad, travelling and attending international schools.

One activity was designed to introduce students to using the Internet to gather data and graph using *MS Excel* (any spreadsheet programme will work). Using the *CIA's Home Page for Kids* site they located and recorded statistical information that would be useful for their research questions. They made pie and bar or column graphs which included proper titles, legends, and the source. This information allowed students to make and support recommendations based on actual data. For example, many students gave advice about which languages the client should learn from finding out the dominant language in the country. Students were asked to include their graphs on the visual aid (poster) they would use during the client meeting. The visual aid also required the nation's name, three pictures downloaded from any computer source, and a sample business card.

A second activity in the computer lab involved writing letters to clients in *MS Word*. Students were introduced to the block business letter format and given specific details that needed to be included in their letters. For example, students introduced themselves, stated their credentials, and enumerated the services they could offer and explained why they should be given the contract to work for their clients. Later, a second business letter was written to the client explaining preparations prior to the meeting. Students identified what the client would learn regarding the project nation and provided logistical information such as date, time, and place of the scheduled meeting. The second business letter is the one that the client read before meeting the consultant on the actual 'Client Meeting Day'.

In preparation for the client meeting and presentations students made business cards using *MS Publisher*. Each designed a unique Logo and created a job title. A scanner was used for hand drawn logos. *MS Publisher* has a business card wizard that helped to automate the design process. Students also made their own nameplates to place on their desks during the client meeting using an *MS Publisher* template designed in-house. It included the GNI logo, their name, title and flag of the country that they represented.

A letter to parents requested their participation in the culminating event. Parents were asked to be clients who were moving to the Middle East and students acted as their Cultural Consultants. Special attention was given to organising consultants with clients – students were not matched with their own parents because of the client-consultant evaluation after the meeting. Staff members were also asked to be clients. Students, dressed professionally for meeting their clients, prepared their work area with poster, nameplate, business cards and necessary papers and a writing utensil. Some students placed jars of candies for their clients and had their business cards in unique holders!

While the consultants were preparing their work area, the clients were asked to read the second business letter from their consultant. They learned what their names would be for the meeting and where they would be pretending to move in the Middle East. The clients also wore nametags. To help clients think of appropriate questions, they were given a question sheet before they meet with consultants.

During the meeting, the consultants presented information using their visual aids and asked selected questions from their questionnaires. Clients asked questions extemporaneously. Consultants verified clients' mailing addresses since they planned to send thank you cards as a follow up to the meeting. Clients were invited to visit other consultants, who were prepared for discussion. Before leaving, the clients were asked to finish the evaluation of their initial consultant. Most clients discussed the evaluation with the consultant before handing the evaluation to the CEO.

A few ESL students who joined the class after the project started were responsible for assisting with preparations for the special day. They acted as administrative assistants during the client meeting. Their responsibilities included welcoming clients, distributing business letters for the clients to read while the consultants were arranging their desks, distributing nametags to the clients, and escorting the clients to their consultants. The administrative assistants also served refreshments during the meeting.

As a challenge project, a few students decided to create a Power Point presentation in lieu of a poster. The project will be modified to incorporate Power Point next year.

Support materials (p68-82)

A. Introduction to the project
B. Client sample questions
C. Client questionnaire
D. Scavenger hunt
E. Documenting sources and the search
F. Memorandum
G. The business card - rough draft
H. Sample name card (originally done in *MS Publisher*)
I. Parent showcase letter
J. Checklist for students
K. Client meeting checklist

Evaluation of Student Achievement

A. Student to student evaluation form
(for use with oral presentations prior to client meetings)

Presenter's Name:_____

Evaluator's Name:_____

Evaluate the presenter for each category on a scale of 1 to 6. (One being the poorest grade, six the highest.)

PRESENTATION

The presenter was prepared to present when asked. It is evident that the presenter practised what he/she would say in front of the class.

      1   2   3   4   5   6

The presenter spoke clearly, used expression, and gestures.

      1   2   3   4   5   6

The presenter provided essential basic facts about the country that she/he studied.

      1   2   3   4   5   6

The presenter included information necessary when moving to a Middle Eastern country.

      1   2   3   4   5   6

He/she showed effort, creativity, and originality in his/her presentation.

      1   2   3   4   5   6

The presenter was able to sufficiently answer reasonable questions.

      1   2   3   4   5   6

The poster had two graphs from Microsoft Excel. The information was relevant and was used in the presentation.

      1   2   3   4   5   6

The poster had three photos, drawn or printed, that depicted life in his/her Middle Eastern country of study.

      1   2   3   4   5   6

The graphs, photos and other information were incorporated in the presentation.

      1   2   3   4   5   6

The poster showed effort, originality, and creativity.

      1   2   3   4   5   6

SCORE_____ (TOTAL 60 POINTS)

B. Client-consultant evaluation form

(for use by the client to provide feedback on the consultant's performance after the meeting)

Name of Cultural Consultant:_____

Project Country:_____

Section:_____

Evaluate the presenter for each category on a scale of 1 to 6. (One being the poorest grade, six the highest.)

The presenter spoke clearly, used expression, and gestures.

      1   2   3   4   5   6

The presenter provided essential basic facts about the country that she/he studied. She/he also included information necessary when moving to a Middle Eastern country.

      1   2   3   4   5   6

He/she showed effort, creativity, and originality in his/her presentation.

      1   2   3   4   5   6

The graphs, photos and other information were explained to you during the presentation.

      1   2   3   4   5   6

The poster showed effort, originality, and creativity.

      1   2   3   4   5   6

The consultant asked questions taken from his/her questionnaire effectively and was able to explain, if necessary, why these questions were asked.

      1   2   3   4   5   6

The consultant was able to satisfactorily answer questions that you asked from the question sheet that was given to you.

      1   2   3   4   5   6

The consultant greeted and spoke to you in a professional way. She/he was prepared for the meeting. The consultant discussed how he/she would follow-up on today's meeting. You received a business card.

      1   2   3   4   5   6

SCORE_____ **(TOTAL 48 POINTS)**

Reflections
How can we help students manage information overload?

Nowadays research is more than looking facts up in a book. It is a process that involves CD-ROMS, the Internet, databanks, and various other information technology resources.

The ultimate goal of this project was to study Middle Eastern geography and culture. The project idea, or 'hook', of using a transition consultant helped to engage international students in the assignment. Global Nomads face challenging lives and have unique experiences as they move from country to country. This project permitted students to also explore these issues as they relate to their own lives. Engagement in the topic proved to be an important deterrent to information overload.

Students also need an effective research strategy to be successful in today's information-rich environment. Several effective research models exist and in duplicating this project it would be helpful to consult one of the following:

INFOZONE at **http://www.assd.winnipeg.mb.ca/infozone**
The Organized Investigator at
http://ctap.fcoe.k12.ca.us/ctap/Info.Lit/Organized.html
The Research Cycle at **http://questioning.org/Q6/research.html**

The first step for students was to formulate a research question or focused topic idea, such as *What information and advice would be useful for a family moving to Iran?* A graphic organiser, such as those designed using *Inspiration 4.0*, is very useful in delineating focus areas and could have been another activity conducted in the computer lab at the end of the research phase of the project, with details added to the chart by the students as illustrated below.

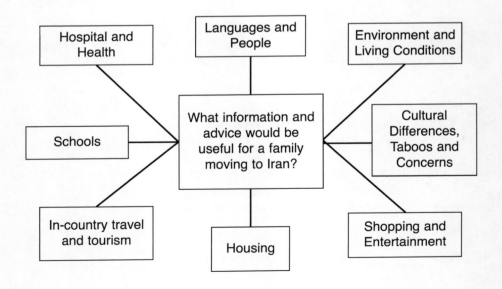

The ideas incorporated in this mind map were generated as part of a brainstorming session during the first orientation day and as a prelude to the research. These focusing techniques built on students' prior knowledge and prepared them for the difficult phase of information searching.

The research process began with a multi-source spiral approach to locating relevant information. The spiralling outward process involved going from highly condensed and organised to more diffuse sources of information. The early phase of research generally offers access to reliable, appropriate and reviewed information. In this case the process started with learning a little about the country from a hard-copy source; generally students chose an encyclopaedia or almanac. This allowed students to begin gathering key-words that would be helpful later in deciding what would be useful information for a family moving to the Middle East. More often it led to questions that could not be answered by using these traditional sources. The spiralling outward process would then incorporate the use of books, magazines and periodicals from the library's general collection. Online access to SIRS and Newsbank facilitated this process. Students progressed to atlas and encyclopaedia CD-ROMs, which led to using the Internet for their spiralling information needs. Middle-school students can be overwhelmed when they search for information online, even when they have followed a spiralling path from print to electronic resources. For this reason, a guided, first search is helpful. Pre-selected Internet sites were compiled on a research web page specific to the Global Nomads, Inc. project. In this case it was added to the 7th grade social studies web site at **http://www.ash.nl/ms/grade7/SubjectAreaSites/7thCurrentEvent.html**

This provided controlled and focused access to the Internet before students went on to using any search engines.

The multi-source spiral approach guided students from print to electronic sources. When they went online they were already focused and had read background information that helped them to select what was relevant. This also helped students to develop an awareness of the complexity of information searching on the web and an opportunity to compare and contrast print and electronic sources.

Support Materials for Chapter Three

Activity :	Global Nomads Inc
Information Literacy Focus:	Using print and electronic resources

A. Introduction to the project: Global Nomads Inc transitions: families on the move

Global Nomads are persons of any age or nationality who have lived a significant part of their developmental years in one or more countries outside their passport country because of a parent's occupation.

As the children of diplomatic, international business, governmental agency, international agency, missionary or military personnel, or indeed of people living internationally-mobile lives for any other professional reason, global nomads share a unique cultural heritage. They typically share similar responses to the benefits and challenges of a childhood abroad.

Global nomads have the opportunity to gain a three dimensional worldview. News reports are more than ink on paper; they recall sights and sounds and smells and feelings. Global nomads know that people different from them share a fundamental humanity. They understand that truth depends in large measure on context.

It is important to help global nomads develop their ability to be at home wherever they may find themselves. Your job is to find the necessary information from your clients in order for them to have a smooth transition into their new countries. You may consider asking the following questions during your meeting:

How many times have you and your family moved nationally or internationally? Where have you lived before and for how long in each place?

How does each family member feel about your move to the Middle East? You can use a scale of 1 to 5 to determine this.

How would you rate your family's good-bye process to your last 'home' on a scale of 1 to 5?

What/who are you leaving behind?

What are the names of your best friends and closest relatives? How will you keep in touch with them?

How would you rate the support network you have here now? How would you rate the support network in place for you in the Middle Eastern country where you will live?

What do your family members enjoy doing in their leisure time?

Are you interested in learning the language of the new country?

Do you need to know where you can find places of worship in the new country?

Possible questions that you should be able to answer are:

What types of schools are suitable for my children? Does the school(s) offer IB? What is the teacher/student ratio? What is the curriculum for various subjects? Does the school offer extra-curricular activities? Which ones? Where is it located in relation to my house? What type of transportation would my child/children be offered to get to and from school?

What type of orientation programme does the community/company offer to new families? What support systems are in place? What kind of support network is in place for the non-working spouse?

Where do most expatriates live?

What types of services are available in my new community? How far is the grocery store? Is there public transportation available? How do I exchange my driver's licence for a local one? How far is the nearest hospital?

Are there any outstanding cultural norms that I should know before I move to the Middle Eastern country?

Ask your clients if they can think of a 'sacred object' that they could bring with them from The Netherlands to the Middle East.

Sacred objects play an important role to help global nomads feel at home wherever they may find themselves. Those objects remind one of family, friends, community, and belonging, and can be slipped into a pocket, taken on an airplane, or placed carefully in a hotel room. Also of critical importance is the capacity to bring effective closure; we can't move forward into a new location unless and until we have said the necessary good-byes. It is vital that in times of transition families attend to the psychosocial dimensions as well as the logistical; it does no good to remember the airplane tickets and the passports if emotional needs are ignored.

Information taken from *ASH Transition Programme Planning Team*, prepared by Barbara F. Schaetti.

B. Client sample questions

Dear Client,
These are possible questions that you may wish to ask your Cultural Consultant during your meeting today.

SCHOOL

What types of schools are suitable for my children?

Does the school(s) offer IB?

What is the teacher/student ratio?

What is the curriculum for various subjects?

Does the school offer extracurricular activities? Which ones?

Where is it located in relation to my house? What type of transportation would my child/children be offered to get to and from school?

WORK/COMMUNITY/HOUSING

What type of orientation programme does the community/company offer to new families? What support systems are in place?

What kind of support network is in place for the non-working spouse?

Where do most expatriates live?

What types of services are available in my new community?

How far is the grocery store?

Is there public transportation available?

How do I exchange my driver's licence for a local one?

How far is the nearest hospital?

Are there any outstanding cultural norms that I should know before I move to the Middle Eastern country?

C. Sample client questionnaire

Name:	Section:	Item:

Client's Family Name:	First name:

Mailing Address:

Tel number:	Fax number:

E-mail address:

Planned departure date:	Intended length of stay:

It is important to help global nomads develop their ability to be at home wherever they may find themselves. Your job is to find the necessary information from your clients in order for them to have a smooth transition to their new country. You may consider the following questions to ask during your meeting:

How many times have you and your family moved nationally or internationally?

Where have you lived before and for how long in each place?

How does each family member feel about your move to the Middle East? You can use a scale of 1 to 5 to determine this._____

How would you rate your family's good-bye process to your last 'home' on a scale of 1 to 5?

What/who are you leaving behind?

What are the names of your best friends and closest relatives? How will you keep in touch with them?

How would you rate the support network you have here now? How would you rate the support network in place for you in the Middle Eastern country where you will live?

What do your family members enjoy doing in their leisure time?

Are you interested in learning the language of the new country?

Do you need to know where you can find places of worship in the new country?

Can you think of a 'sacred object' (*see page 69*) that you could take from The Netherlands (or from the country where you now live) to the Middle East. Why would you choose this object?

Also include in the questionnaire space for:

Additional questions

Helpful web sites

Planned follow-up to the meeting

D. Scavenger hunt

Name: _____   Country: _____   Item: _____

Global Nomads Inc

Congratulations! You have been hired as a Cultural Consultant for an agency that specialises in helping families make the difficult adjustments when they move internationally. You are going to be the specialist for the country, _____. Later you will make contact with a specific company in _____ that will require your services. Before you take your first job, we want you to familiarise yourself with the resources you can use to find valuable information about your country. Up-to-date information resources from the Global Nomad Library include book sources, CD-ROMs and the Internet.

YOU'RE GOING ON A SCAVENGER HUNT!

You must find the following basic information about your country,

_____

By circling the appropriate letter, indicate whether you found the information from:

  a book source (B); CD-ROM (C); a specific Internet site (I); from a Search Engine on the Internet (S).

You must use each resource at least five times.

B C I S	Capital City
B C I S	Principal Language(s)
B C I S	Population
B C I S	Area in squared km
B C I S	Population density
B C I S	Birth rate per 100 people
B C I S	Death rate per 100 people
B C I S	Natural population growth per 100 people (Births-Deaths=%Gain)
B C I S	Time zone
B C I S	Describe natural vegetation
B C I S	Average precipitation from November through April mm
B C I S	Average precipitation from May through October mm
B C I S	Average temperature in January °F
B C I S	Average temperature in July °F
B C I S	Major religion(s) - give percentages
B C I S	Food availability (daily calories per person)
B C I S	Cropland per capita (acres per person)
B C I S	Available health care (people per physician)
B C I S	Percentage of population with safe drinking water
B C I S	Life expectancy in years
B C I S	AIDS (Acquired Immune Deficiency Syndrome - reported cases per 1 million people)
B C I S	Major cause(s) of death
B C I S	Adult literacy (% of people 15 or older)
B C I S	Type of government
B C I S	Member of the following International Organizations

List at least six other pieces of information about _____. Find at least two pieces of information from two book sources, two from CD-ROMs and two from the Internet. Be sure to indicate where you found your information.

B C I S
B C I S
B C I S
B C I S
B C I S
B C I S

E. Documenting sources and the search

From the library:
a. List three books that include information about your country. Include the book title and the call number.

b. Write a sentence that explains how you accessed the information from the library. (How did you find the books that contain information about your country?)

From an Internet site:
a. Name at least three full web site addresses that you consulted to learn more about your country.

b. Write a sentence that explains how you accessed the information on the Internet.

From CD-ROMs:
a. Name the CD-ROM software.

b. Write a sentence that explains how you accessed the information from a CD-ROM.

F. Memorandum

To: Grade 7 Student
From: Nicole Whelan, CEO, Global Nomads Inc
Date: December 7, 2000
RE: Business cards

Though Global Nomads Inc is just seeing its first days of business, I am pleased to say that I have received many phone calls and other expressions of interest in the type of cultural expertise that we will soon be able to offer. It appears that we will need to get business cards made immediately. Companies or families in your focus country will be able to direct their business and concerns to the right person. When you design your own business card please observe the basic requirements listed below.

G. The Business Card

Requirements:
Size – 5½cm x 9 cm
Colour – any light coloured background will work
Company name with logo of your design
Contact information
Your name
Your title (Expert in _____ Culture, or _____ Cultural Consultant)
Address, post code, country
Phone number with country code and city code
Fax number with country code and city code
E-mail address

You may use the corporate headquarters address for your card:
Global Nomads Inc
Corporate Headquarters, Room [Number]
[Address/contact details of school]

GOOD LUCK!   I'm looking forward to seeing your completed card in time for the next busy workday, [date].

Use the following page to draw a rough draft of your business card.

Business card: Rough draft

Provide students with an outline of business card dimensions (*eg* 5½cm x 9cm).

We will be using [name of publishing software] to make our business cards. Please have your original handmade logos on clean white paper ready for scanning.

H. Sample name card

Jane Jones

I. Parent Showcase Letter

[date]

Dear Parent(s),

In Social Studies class we have examined many issues regarding the Middle East today. You are invited to learn more about your child's work on [date], during Social Studies class. Please come to room [room number] at [time] until [time]. Refreshments will be served.

As a final project for this unit of study, each student has become an *expert* for one country in the Middle East or neighbouring area. Each will present the information he/she learned by acting as a Cultural Consultant. He/she will help you, their *client*, with your *pretend* move to the Middle East. Each student has prepared a presentation with the information that you would need if you moved to this part of the world. He/she will ask questions regarding your *pretend* move. Creative fictitious answers are expected! He/she will answer possible questions that you may have as well.

We will begin the period with a brief explanation of the consultant/client meeting(s). Next, each student will meet with his/her client. Then, feel free to meet with other students to learn more about the Middle East. Please support this seventh grade Social Studies project! I look forward to seeing you on Thursday.

Sincerely,

[name of teacher]
[Grade ? Social Studies Teacher]

✂————————————————————————————————

Please cut and return the bottom portion of this letter to [name of teacher] by [date] indicating whether you will be available to attend this Social Studies showcase. For planning purposes, I need an idea of who is attending since each student is required to meet with at least one client, so it is important to return this form for our planning purposes.

Student's Name: _____Section: _____

Mother/guardian will attend: _____ Yes   _____ No
Father/guardian will attend: _____ Yes   _____ No

Parent/guardian signature: _____

J. Checklist for students

Name: Country: Item:

The Global Nomads Inc project requires the following:

1. Memo to [name of teacher], CEO of Global Nomads regarding contract work and preparations that you are doing before meeting with families who are moving to your project country.

    Due: _____

2. A poster with information on your project country. Your poster should include at least two graphs, one pie and one bar or column graph from Excel. Have at least three drawings or photos from your country. Display one of your business cards on your poster.

    Due: _____

3. A block letter to inform your client of what you have been doing to prepare for your meeting. You must have at least three paragraphs.

    Due: _____

    1ST PARAGRAPH: Include your title, background, and what you are doing to prepare for your meeting together.

    2ND PARAGRAPH: Include the type of information that will be learned regarding the country where he/she/they is/are moving.

    3RD PARAGRAPH: Include meeting details such as the date, time, and place. State that you will be able to answer questions at that time and closing.

4. A three to five minute presentation on your project country. You should explain what it would be like to move to this Middle Eastern country. Provide information your audience would need if they moved to that country. You will present your information twice. One presentation will be in front of the class and the second to your client(s).

    Your Class Presentation is on _____

    Your Client(s) Presentation is on _____

K. Client meeting checklist

Name: _____ Section: _____ Item: _____

By [date]:

☐ Give *two copies* of your *block letter* with the *official letterhead* to [name of teacher]

☐ Place *one copy* of the block letter *in your notebook* (Have an extra copy of the block letter for your client meeting)

☐ Make a *name tag for your client* and pass it in to [name of teacher] (attached with a paperclip to the copies of your block letter)

For your client meeting on [date]:

☐ Dress professionally

☐ Place a *name plate* on your desk

☐ Place *business cards* on your desk

☐ Hang a poster in a visible place for use during presentation

☐ Have *client questionnaire* on your desk

☐ Have an *answer sheet* to possible client questions on your desk

☐ Have a *copy of block letter* on your desk

☐ Have your *presentation note cards* or *papers* on your desk

☐ Have a *writing utensil* (pen) on your desk!

☐ Have *blank paper* on your desk to take notes

Recommended web sites

American School in The Hague: Global Nomads Homepage
http://www.ash.nl/ms/grade7/gni/gni_homepage.html

American School in The Hague: Subject Area Sites
http://www.ash.nl/ms/grade7/SubjectAreaSites/7thCurrentEvent.html

Ask Jeeves for Kids
http://www.ajkids.com/

CIA's Homepage for Kids
Provides access to the *World Fact Books* and a rich resource of information useful for this project.
http://www.cia.gov/cia/ciakids/index.html

Google – search engine
http://www.google.com

INFOZONE
http://www.assd.winnipeg.mb.ca/infozone

Kid's Almanac, atlas, dictionary and encyclopedia
http://factmonster.com

The Organized Investigator
http://ctap.fcoe.k12.ca.us/ctap/Info.Lit/Organized.html

Outpost Expatriate Information Centre
An independent network of information centers around the world, created to provide practical information to expatriates and their families. This site contains an extensive listing of worldwide resources, including those on the World Wide Web, for expatriates both at pre-departure stage and for settling in.
http://www.outpostexpat.nl/

The Research Cycle
http://questioning.org/Q6/research.html

Chapter Four

Survival Strategies for Reading Non-Fiction Text

Activity:	Emergency Rescue Package
Level:	Grades 4-9
Interdisciplinary Action:	History
Information Literacy Focus:	Reading for understanding
Project Designer	Ali Wills, Stephanie Vernon, International School of Monaco

Project description

Teachers of social studies and the sciences are already aware that their students struggle with reading and understanding non-fiction. They observe the symptoms of reading dysfunction when their students copy chunks of text wholesale, indulge in word-for-word translation (that is, they substitute another word of their choosing for each word of the text). It is evident when students are unable to recognise when a text is relevant or when they have found enough material. Teachers will also tell you that students complain that they are unable to find any material at all, anywhere. Librarians have often heard the refrains, "This book doesn't have any information" or "This library doesn't have any good books".

Emergency Rescue Package arose out of a history research essay on 'Current Conflicts' as students exhibited distress when reading non-fiction text. Each student had selected a modern conflict to research. Finding ways to read and understand non-fiction texts took place during English and history lessons. Support was designed to help students recognise the variety of problems posed by reading long pieces of non-fiction text; to understand the processes involved and to sample different ways of decoding such texts.

Discussions had already taken place with the history teacher on the research project he was setting. Part of these discussions concerned the continuing teaching of research skills by the librarian. The problems of recognising relevance and understanding text were touched upon as students struggled with new approaches to teaching and learning. The next person to be approached was the Head of English. She was keen to take part in anything that might improve her students' reading skills and agreed to set aside three hours of English lessons. She could see the way in which this work would directly relate to the background research that students were now being asked to undertake in English and was more than willing to work in partnership on the project. The time chosen was two weeks into the students' history research. They had been given a month in which to complete a 1,000-word essay.

Lesson one

Lesson one (one hour) began by making the students understand where their difficulties with the texts they were encountering lay. This was done in the following ways: Students had to 'Think at the Point of the Pen'. This involved continuous writing, without stopping, without worrying about spelling, punctuation or handwriting and, in the case of ESL students, writing in their primary language. They were given a topic and told to write down every thought they had, but also to include such things as 'I wish I was at home' or 'I don't know what to write', if that was what they were thinking. They were encouraged to stay on the topic. They were reassured that they were the only people who would read their writings. Students need practice with this activity. It is a very important way of allowing students to relax enough to be able to recall information and to recognise how much knowledge they already possess. It is worth persevering with this kind of thinking-writing whenever opportunity allows.

The title given for the writing was 'Problems with my History Research Topic'. The title was purposefully wide and obvious in order to give an opportunity for other problems to surface. Students were then told to write for five minutes without stopping. When they had finished writing they read through and underlined or circled anything they wanted to share with the class. This was the basis for class brainstorming on general problems. The focus then narrowed to understanding non-fiction texts once they had found them either in the library or on the Internet. A page of fiction was read to them and they were asked to predict the possible next events and to explain the text to each other. They were able to do this.

Next, a page of a history text taken from a general history book rather than a school text was read out loud and students were again asked to predict events. They found this almost impossible; they couldn't predict and had great difficulty explaining anything about the text. A general class discussion of the differences between the two texts followed. The layout of a page of their geography textbook was compared with the page of the history text and differences and potential problems discussed (*eg*, the way in which text was broken by pictures and diagrams in the geography text and the unbroken prose of the history text. The class defined characteristics of fiction on the board, followed by characteristics of non-fiction. Students noted these alongside their writing. The lesson finished with a discussion of why fiction was easier to read, linked to the ideas on the board and some suggestions from both teacher and librarian about the use of story in everyday life.

Students were given the same historical article for homework, asked to read it, underline words and phrases they didn't understand and write at least five questions they would like to ask about the text.

Lesson two

Lesson two reviewed what students had covered in the last lesson. The characteristics of fiction and non-fiction were noted on the board as students recapitulated the final discussion of the first session and used their notes.

Students made the following points about non-fiction texts:

- They tend to contain unfamiliar, subject-specific, technical terms.
- There are whole pages of unbroken prose instead of the small pieces of text in textbooks, to which students were accustomed.
- The tone and style are unfamiliar.
- There is a lack of narrative – it's not story telling.
- The usual clues found in fiction are absent.
- Concentration is difficult, because of all of the above, making understanding of the piece difficult.

Next, the homework article was discussed. The words/phrases they hadn't understood, and the questions they had written, were placed on the board. The class discussed the questions and offered answers. This is not as long a process as it might appear because students replicated questions and often provided answers for each other. Also, the act of phrasing the question can begin the process of understanding, unless it is a purely subject-centred reference. In this case phrases referring to the Monroe Doctrine caused problems.

In order to give students as wide a variety of techniques as possible for studying texts, the class was divided into four groups. All were given the same historical text related to one of their research topics. However, each group was given a different activity, as follows:

- The article was cut into sections, and any headings or sub-headings removed. The students were asked to put it back together again so that it made sense. (It is important that a few of the cut sections come from a different photocopy otherwise students are tempted to put them together like a jigsaw – matching cut edge to cut edge!)
- Students were given the entire article but had to write a sub-heading for each paragraph that encapsulated the meaning of the paragraph.
- Students had to underline the topic sentence in each paragraph.
- Students wrote a series of questions on the article for others to answer. (They had to know the answers!)
- Five major points had to be highlighted. These were then used to write a brief commentary on the article.

These activities were repeated with other texts. Again, it's important to ensure that the pieces they are reading relate to their topics. In this way they can see how the activities are helping them to read and understand something that has immediacy.

For homework a further selection of historical texts was made available and students selected material that was relevant to their research topics. They had to use any one of the techniques practised in the lesson to read and understand the text. Understanding would be demonstrated by explaining their piece to the group and pointing out how it might be relevant to their research.

Lesson Three

Students met in their previous groups for lesson three and, in turn, explained the main points in the text they had read and its relevance to their research. Students were then asked which activity they had chosen to help them understand their text. These were written on the board. Patterns were identified and a general discussion took place that was linked to the problems of reading non-fiction that had been identified in the first lesson, and the ways in which the various activities had helped to overcome these problems. Emphasis was given to the importance of recognising the way in which each individual read a text and the activity that was most helpful to each of them. A number of students had found that putting the cut-up article together had been helpful but hadn't done this with the homework text because "It seemed stupid!" This kind of comment can lead directly to the most important stage: consideration of how meaning is constructed when reading. When reading a text that has been dissected students are consciously aware of the way in which they are forced to continually read and re-read. The have to check meanings in final sentences in paragraphs and then fit them with opening sentences of other paragraphs. They are actively re-constructing the text as they are constructing its meaning.

In order for this project to work successfully, enough time must be given to it. In this case three hours of English were needed. One problem that must be faced is the time allocation: because the project is not attached to one particular subject, departments may be reluctant to give up curriculum time. However, the skills that students need must be taught in context so that they can see their relevance. It is essential that activities described here are anchored in a current subject-based research project.

Post-activity

The most important post-activity is ensuring that all members of staff know about the project and why it took place. It is often assumed that teachers provide students with skills and techniques for dealing with texts and that the activities described in the project are the common currency of all classrooms. The time it takes for students to master complex skills that require experience with text is often underestimated. Like other information literacy skills, mastering non-fiction text is teachable! Talking to other Heads of Department, to Principals, giving an Inset workshop at Heads of Department meetings are ways in which discussion can begin. Students' problems with searching for research material, recognising relevant information and understanding what they have read are constant challenges. When librarians teach information literacy skills they are also creating opportunities to talk with teachers about reading instruction in context.

Support materials

Texts from history books as well as newspaper reports and articles from Internet sources were selected and photocopied so that each student would have one copy of each. All of these were closely related to the research projects that the students had chosen. In this case there were texts on the USA's relationship with Cuba, on China and Tibet, on the conflict in Northern Ireland, and Kosovo. It was important to the success of the work that each student recognised the importance of relating to the text on a personal level of information need.

Evaluation of student achievement

These three lessons were designed to be exploratory: to help students begin to think about their own reading practices when faced with lengthy non-fiction texts and to experiment with various helpful strategies. Assessment of the project was based on student feedback about what they had found illuminating and useful.

In lesson three students returned to a personal piece of writing as a self-assessment. They were asked to write about the discoveries they had made about their own reading practices when dealing with non-fiction and the activities that had helped them most. This writing was handed in for teachers to read and handed back for students to keep in their files. Reading Workshop, discussed in Chapter 9, and journal writing, with its running dialogue between teacher and student, are useful for ensuring that the strategies described in this chapter become continuous and ongoing. The portfolio, an integral part of Reading Workshop, is perhaps the most ideal instrument to show progress in reading over time. Portfolios also provide opportunities for self-reflection and evaluation, adding a metacognitive level to reading improvement.

Reflection

The literacy part of information literacy

As the demand for authentic, student-centred learning grows, more departments are setting research projects for students. The assumption seems to be that once a child can read, then, as long as the text is not too advanced, they can read anything. This is apparently not true. It is even less true of the level of text students are using when they research on the Internet. With the emphasis on using electronic resources students are accessing all kinds of texts which make many demands on their reading and comprehension skills.

Teachers are aware that students need the know-how to assess Internet sites for relevance, reliability and the like but this ignores the fact, indeed presupposes, that in order to make any kind of meaningful assessment students must be able to read and understand what they have found. Even a cursory survey of the kinds of non-fiction reading students meet in subject classrooms in their text books will show that it is extraordinarily undemanding and doesn't in the least prepare them for dealing with the kinds of texts they will find when they search electronically. Social studies and Science texts, the most common forms of non-fiction texts found in schools, have pages of text broken up by diagrams, photos, illustrations and questions. The paragraphs tend to be neatly sub-headed, introducing the main idea of the next paragraph.

In noting this as an area for critical appraisal we are not suggesting that such texts should be made more obscure and difficult. What we are saying is that students have limited experience of dealing with complex texts. Throughout their school lives, students meet pages of unbroken text mainly in fiction. However, fiction makes demands on the reader in a different kind of way. Because we live our lives through story and narrative even a text by someone as difficult as Henry James has a certain air of predictability about it. Students know that certain kinds of events will take place. Because of experience with fiction they can make a number of guesses as to how the story might unfold.

Although they may feel threatened by sophisticated language and complex sentence structure in fiction reading, they know the world they are inhabiting and they know the kinds of clues to look for. This is not true of non-fiction. Students have no signposts to guide them. They may be dealing for the first time with a subject they know very little about rather than life experiences rooted in emotion, such as death, love and hate or family and relationships. They must wait and wait for understanding and this delayed understanding can be very threatening. The normal clues that they are used to are missing in non-fiction. There is very little narrative curiosity to keep them going unless the subject is one they are deeply interested in. Here students may persevere with a difficult and demanding text. In non-fiction, there will inevitably be references to people and events about which they know nothing, such as dealing with the relationship between the USA and Cuba and finding references to the Monroe Doctrine, or reading a science text and finding casual mention of chaos theory. Students can find such references stumbling blocks.

Students need on-going help to recognise what they are dealing with and how to overcome such problems. The project described in this chapter was not designed to be a one-off project. It was designed as an emergency rescue package that would be applied in an ongoing and continuous process of giving students the tools and insights they need to read demanding non-fiction texts. Ideally all the techniques and activities outlined would be part of the classroom teacher's armour and part of all project work that was resource-based; a way to approach texts in subject areas.

Information and communication technology is moving across and through the curriculum because all teachers are being made aware of the need to make students confident and flexible users of technology. However, our students will continue to plagiarise and use sound bytes of knowledge if their comprehension skills remain immature, aggravated by a dearth of coping strategies. Bringing students to the library is not enough. Giving them lists of vocabulary words is not enough. Even providing support materials such as graphic organisers and rubrics is not enough if students do not understand what they are reading.

An authentic assessment tool that supports the ongoing process of developing literacy is the portfolio. Selected work can be excerpted from library units and assignments, or from activities, such as the ones described in *Emergency Rescue Package*, so that students can see their progress over time. Portfolios are excellent vehicles for weaving self-evaluation and reflection into reading progress through students' reflective writing entries for each work selected for the portfolio. Examples of types of student work generated by library and resource-based assignments are listed below. These examples of portfolio entries lend themselves to exercises, such as those described in this chapter, that help students confront and engage with non-fiction text. For example, ongoing journal entries that address the difficulties students experience when reading non-fiction, accompanied by excerpts which were particularly challenging, track student progress over time.

Examples of criteria for student-selected work for portfolios

- Early/Later pieces
- Unedited versions/Revisions
- High/Low grades
- Best/Worst work
- Easy/Difficult pieces
- Individual/Group projects, assignments
- Pivotal pieces
- Companion pieces
- Journal entries, excerpts
- Pieces to balance the portfolio (*eg* subjects represented)
- Pieces showing development, changes
- Published pieces (*eg* intranet, school newspaper, library)
- Reading reactions
- Writings for a variety of audiences
- Writings for a variety of purposes

Maintaining an information literacy portfolio, with the emphasis on literacy across disciplines implies a grade level initiative and the participation, if not leadership, of the librarian. Establishing an information literacy focus for each grade level, based on the academic needs that can be distilled from projects and resource-based activities that are already established gives the librarian opportunities to heighten awareness of the importance of reading strategies.

Recommended web sites

Portfolios
Guidelines for Portfolio Assessment in teaching English
http://www.w-angle.galil.k12.il/call/portfolio/default.html

Portfolio Assessment Model for ESL
http://www.ncbe.gwu.edu/miscpubs/jeilms/vol13/portfo13.htm

Reading Strategies
Curriculum Associates: Reading Strategies for Non-fiction (Grades 1-8)
http://www.curriculumassociates.com/publications/readingnon.shtml

Mind Tools-Communication-Using reading strategies to read more quickly and effectively. Go to the following links: *Active Reading; Knowing How to Read Different Sorts of Material*
http://www.mindtools.com/rdstratg.html

Study Guides for testing, reading, writing and classroom participation
Look at Reading Skills- Reading difficult material for strategies
http://www.iss.stthomas.edu/studyguides

Chapter Five

Looking for the Smoking Gun: Collecting Data

Activity:	Smoking Project
Level:	Grade 8-10
Interdisciplinary Action:	Science, English, maths, computers
Information Literacy Focus:	Collecting information/data; analysis
Project Designer:	John Cordwell, Frankfurt International School

Project description

The decision to smoke, or not to smoke, engages pre-teens and lingers throughout adolescence for many. Beneath the surface of the question are complex issues of identity and peer acceptance. Placing the question in the scientific context of a health issue is a solid academic approach. Empowering students to become researchers who gather facts and statistics and talk with their peers and adults about smoking addresses emotional and social aspects of the issue. Students examine the question, 'Does Smoking Affect Your Health?' They collect information from secondary resources and data from people, using questionnaires and interviews. They also collect data in the form of statistics gathered from research studies. Activities are designed to engage students in the following activities, each of which becomes a chapter in the booklets they create:

Research the history of smoking using print and electronic resources;

Perform a scientific experiment using the 'smoking machine';

Survey students and teachers who are smokers using a questionnaire;

Results of the surveys are entered into a database which student use to analyse data;

Collect statistics and current research on smoking that are entered into spreadsheets to create various types of graphs;

Draw conclusions, based on the evidence collected in preceding chapters, about the research question, 'Does smoking affect your health?'

This project has opportunities for students to use three computer applications: word processing, spreadsheets and databases. If the unit is integrated with technology in the school's computer lab, Help Sheets that contain explicit directions, with screen captures can be made available for those students who need them.

When students design and analyse their questionnaires and when they use statistics for evidence, the Maths teacher can provide support. A lesson in descriptive statistics covering the concepts of sample, mode, median and mean would be helpful for students.

The English teacher can support the writing of the booklet, applying the writing process and a writing rubric developed by the English department that identifies the standards for good writing and descriptors what writing, on at least three levels of performance, looks like relative to the standards.

Social Studies, or Humanities, teachers can help with research on the history of smoking in developed and developing countries.

The support materials that follow were developed by the Science teacher to guide students through gathering data and writing the booklet. The librarian designed the student packet to guide students through gathering information from print and electronic resources.

To view an exemplar of a student's Smoking Project, go to **http://www.ecis.org**

Support materials (p98-108)

A. Help sheet for chapter one of smoking booklet: History/Trends in Smoking 1900-1998

B. Help sheet for chapter two of smoking booklet: The Smoking Machine Experiment

C. Help sheet for chapter three of smoking booklet: Diseases Caused by Smoking

D. Help sheets for chapter four of smoking booklet: The Questionnaire and the Database

E. Making a database

F. Help sheet for chapter five of smoking booklet: Drawing Conclusions

G. Help sheet for writing and completing your smoking booklet

H. Library packet
1. Where do I look in the library for information?
2. Timeline of the history of smoking
3. Table of statistics
4. Bibliography chart

Evaluation of Student Achievement

Smoking project rubric

	INFORMATION RETRIEVAL	RESEARCH	COMPUTER SKILLS/WORD PROCESSING	COMPUTER SKILLS/SPREAD SHEETS	TECHNOLOGY / ORGANISATIONAL SKILLS
4	• searched in SIRS, Facts on File and Readers' Guide • retrieved relevant information on three smoking issues • information was timely (two years or less)	• took shopping list notes on who, what, when, why and how on the graphic organiser kept complete • bibliography chart of three sources	• Word Processing in font 12 using appropriate formatting of text • inserted original drawings from Draw or Paintbrush • used clip art to cut and paste graphics	• two charts showing given statistics; appropriate graph type chosen for data display • appropriate title for chart • labelled axes • proper notation for percentages, etc • legend • colours chosen to enhance the relationships among data	• presents a floppy disk, in good condition containing one file collated from the files in which data was held in the F drive • disk is labelled with name of file, student's name and section • project presented on time
3	• searched in two databases • retrieved relevant information on two or three smoking issues • information was timely (two years or less)	• shopping list notes on graphic organiser incomplete for who, what, where, when, why and how • bibliography for issues incomplete	• font size 12 for most of text • inserted drawing for lab report fragmented, no colour • used clipart for other pictures • appropriate formatting of text, same format used for headings, labels	• two charts with appropriate type chosen displays data appropriately • title • labels • labelled axis • colours show relationships	• floppy disk in good condition • two or more files on disk • disk labelled with file names, student name and section • presented on time
2	• searched two databases • retrieved relevant articles and/or issues • some information was more than two years old	• shopping list notes do not identify all facts • graphic organiser partly used • bibliography incomplete	• incorrect font size for body of text • formatting of text, headings inappropriate • incomplete drawings/ used clipart only	• one or more charts • inappropriate data display • inappropriate title • some labels missing • no values given for chart • colours inappropriate to show relationships	• floppy disk in satisfactory condition • contains numerous files – not collated • disk labelled with names of relevant files, student name, section • presented on time
1	• searched in only one database • retrieved one article on smoking • information was more than two years	• notes are too wordy; do not identify the facts- who, what, where, when, why • graphic organiser missing or headings ignored • bibliography chart missing or incomplete	• Word Processing in incorrect font size • inappropriate formatting of text • no graphics or drawings	• one or no chart • inappropriate graph type chosen • inappropriate title for chart • no data labels • no labelled axes, no legend • no proper notation for percentages etc • colours chosen ineffective to show relationships	• presents a floppy disk, in poor condition • disk contains numerous files • disk is poorly labelled with name of file, student's name and section • project presented late

Smoking project rubric

	SCIENCE SKILLS/ PRESENTATION	SCIENCE SKILLS/SURVEY	SCIENCE SKILLS/CONTENT	SCIENCE SKILLS/ANALYSIS
4	• lab report word-processed and including diagram drawn using Draw or Paintbrush • lab report includes all required sections with appropriate headings • see standards for Word Processing	• survey questions generate relevant data • three age groups were surveyed • answers to survey questions recorded accurately, and appropriately	• from half to full page discussion of current smoking issues • discussion includes supporting details from the notes	• relates the results of the lab report, graphs, current issues research and the survey to the question, 'Does Smoking Affect Your Health?' • one to one and a half pages long
3	• lab report word processed, incomplete diagram drawn using Draw or Paintshop • lab report contains all required sections with appropriate headings but not necessarily in order • see standards for Word Processing	• most data relevant from survey questions • three groups surveyed, data recorded accurately • long answers to questions recorded	• half to one page discussion of current issues • smoking issues discussed separately • some reference to notes, supporting data	• relates the results of any three of lab report, graphs, current issues and survey questions in discussion of question 'Does smoking affect your health?' • one to one and a half pages long
2	• lab report word processed, diagram drawn using clipart • lab report includes most sections, no section headings • see standards for Word Processing	• survey questions from two groups only • data poorly recorded • some data irrelevant • short answers, not enough information	• half page discussion only • smoking issues discussed in one paragraph or as separate smoking issues • few supporting details from notes	• uses only results from two of lab report, current issues, graphs and survey questions to discuss the question of 'Does smoking affect your health?' • one page long
1	• lab report incomplete poor quality or no diagram drawn • see standards for Word Processing	• survey questions incomplete • one age group surveyed • answers to survey questions irrelevant • answers to survey questions poorly recorded	• less than a half page discussion of current smoking issues • no supporting details from notes	• refers to only one of lab report, current issues, graphs or survey questions in discussion of question 'Does smoking affect your health?' • less than one page long

Reflection

Reporting v researching

The research assignment operates on the report level when student involvement is limited to information gathering, usually demonstrated by reading and taking notes. Reporting has masqueraded as researching for so long that the terms are used interchangeably. While 'doing a report' can be an appropriate fact-finding exercise for short-term assignments, it has been over-prescribed, eating up time for learning and practising the thinking skills required by authentic research. Students express dislike for research when, in fact, they dislike doing reports. A study of ninth graders revealed, 'The student perception of doing research was writing a grammatically correct report that was well presented and provided other people's answers to someone else's question' (Gordon, 1996, p.32). Students expressed negative connotations for research: it was described as 'one of the trials and tribulations of going to school'. Research was seen as an addition to schoolwork and in competition with other assignments. '... we could actually be learning other things in math. We could be learning real things'. Go to the ECIS web site at **www.ecis.org** to view the full-text article, *Is Fish a Vegetable?: A Qualitative Study of a Ninth Grade Research Project*.

Bogus research assignments lead students to perceive library time as an extension of teacher and textbook dependent classroom paradigms. Implicit in the report assignment is an underestimation of what students can do, sending a clear message to them that they are passive recipients. Influenced by authoritarian, top-down models of learning, students value what teachers say rather than what they discover for themselves. The reticence of teachers to take time for 'research' discredits library-based research as a teaching strategy.

Students accommodate teachers' low expectations with disappointing results. Even when there is no intent to copy 'word for word' many papers are the product of cutting and pasting information: they contain little creativity and virtually no discovery that has been tested, analysed and internalised by the learner. Easily subverted assignments, with requirements that can be bought for $50 on the Internet, persist in an electronic age that offers an information and data rich environment.

Defining standards for researching in the context of a project is a good way to raise students' awareness what it means to 'do research'. The rubric, which can be a collaborative exercise of teacher and students, teacher-authored, or student-authored, highlights the standards, or criteria that will be assessed. Rubrics can be used by teachers to grade students, by students to grade other students in a peer review, or by students to self-evaluate. In the case of The Smoking Project described in this chapter, a teacher-authored and administered rubric best suited assessment needs. The emphasis was on science content (*eg*, presentation and analysis) and information literacy (*eg,* technology skills and research). In Chapters 7 and 8 examples of rubrics used for self-evaluation and peer review can be found.

In addition to identifying the foci of the unit in terms of importance, students also benefit from a rubric's descriptors, accompanied by ratings of excellent, good, fair and poor work. When grades are needed these ratings can correspond to letter or number grades, but the emphasis should always be on the substantive feedback that rubrics provide to help students improve their performance.

Rubrics are excellent tools for practising the same evaluation skills that figure so prominently in doing research. They support students who are learning how to be evaluators by:

Using the learning task, or assignment as the grist for assessment, thereby reinforcing the requirements and procedures that define the task. Students place more importance on process, rather than product, when the task, rather than a test, becomes the assessment instrument.

Promoting authentic learning tasks that require students to perform as researchers, using the tools of the expert, rather than as students who are 'looking things up'.

Inviting students to become part of the assessment process, encouraging them to self-assess.

Maintaining focus on content and performance standards rather than grades and tests.

Ensuring student accountability for the standards outlined in the rubric, which can address process as well as product.

Visit the web sites listed at the end of the Support Materials for more information about rubrics.

References

Gordon, C (1996), 'Is fish a vegetable?' A qualitative study of a ninth grade research project, *School Library Media Quarterly*, 25(1), 27-33.

Support Materials
for Chapter Five

Activity: Top Secret

Information Literacy Focus: Display and analysis of
                                            information

A. Help sheet for chapter one of smoking booklet: History/Trends in Smoking 1900-2000

Suggestions for Note Taking

How would you describe the changes in attitudes about smoking during this century in the developed countries?

Why do you think smoking was very popular between 1958 and 1983 in these countries?

How do you account for the sharp increase in smoking from 1939 to 1945 in these countries?

Why do you think there was a sharp decrease in smoking in the 1980s in developed countries?

How do smoking patterns differ in developing countries? Why do you think it is different from the patterns you noted in developed nations?

B. Help sheet for chapter two of smoking booklet: The Smoking Machine Experiment

1. Draw a full page, coloured diagram of the smoking machine apparatus and label its parts.

2. Make note of your observations, including the following:
    Describe how the apparatus looked at the start of the experiment. (Include colour of the cotton wool, the cleanliness of the tubes and test tube, the smell of the apparatus, the smell of the surrounding air.)

Describe how the apparatus looked at the end of the experiment.

Compare the cotton wool, the insides of the tubes, the smell of the apparatus and the air.

Make a list of all the products you saw being produced by burning cigarettes.

The experiment shows the condition of the apparatus after two or three cigarettes were smoked. What do you think the apparatus would look like after 20 cigarettes had been smoked?

What would the apparatus look like after smoking 20 cigarettes every day for ten years?

Do you think this build up of poisons would shorten your life? Why?

Write two or more sentences about how you felt when you saw the results of the experiment.

C. Help sheet for chapter three of smoking booklet: Diseases Caused by Smoking

1 Write a paragraph, based on your research, about each smoking-related disease. You will word process your work. Suggestions:

Use the library sources of information listed in your packet.

You should include emphysema, lung cancer, bronchitis, heart disease.

Draw a diagram showing where the disease affects the body.

2. Find out about the trends in smoking-related diseases during the century, 1900-1998. Write a few sentences describing the trends. Suggestions:

The librarian has some information on this. She has a folder in the library that contains statistics that will help you find the trends in smoking-related diseases.

Make notes and gather statistics ready for making a line chart.

Add the information to your line chart about smoking trends.

Remember to save the file under another name as this will be 'chart 2'.

The x-axis could show four different decades.

Include the statistics for lung cancer and heart disease. Do these trends help to answer your research question, Does smoking affect your health?

D. Help sheets for chapter four of smoking booklet: The Questionnaire and the Database

Suggestions for questions you could ask students and teachers in your survey:

What is your age? Grade?

Male or female?

Do you smoke?

How old were for you when you started smoking?

How many cigarettes do you smoke a day?

Why did you start smoking?

Why do you continue to smoke?

Have you noticed any health effects from smoking?

Do your parents smoke?

How does smoking help you?

What do you like about smoking?

Suggestions for analysing the data you collect from your questionnaire:

What percentage of the school population smokes?

What is the average age the people in your school start to smoke?

What is the average number of cigarettes people in your school smoke?

What are the words that appear over and over in people's responses to a certain question? (*eg* for the eighth question, 65% of respondents used the word 'cough'.)

Make a chart and at the top of each column write a question from your questionnaire.

Record the answers from you questionnaire in each column and look for repetitions and patterns.

See chapter 7, *Students as Authentic Researchers: Upgrading the Research Paper*, for support materials which outline how to design and administer questionnaires, interviews, respondent profiles and letters of informed consent. These materials are appropriate for grades 9-12 and can be adapted for middle school students.

E. Making a database

1. Write in the field names or headings you will use based on your questions in the survey. Example: Name, Age, Grade, When started, Reason for starting, How many/day, Health.

For some of the fields it is convenient to use a code.

Example: Why did you start to smoke?

A = my friends smoked

B = it made me feel grown-up

C = my brother smokes

D = my parents smoke

E = my parents would not let me smoke

The letters, or codes, will make it easier to enter respondents answers in the database and the computer can count how many started smoking because their friends smoked by counting the number of As in that column.

Example of a database on smoking

Last Name	Grade	Began Smoking	Starting Age	No.of yrs	Reasons	No. per day	Health
MsTeach	t	1971	22	27	E	20	ABC
Pete	12	1997	11	01	BE	01	ABC
Susan	10	1996	13	02	AE	03	BCE
Fred	11	1995	13	03	AB	20	ACD
Ms Hook	t	1967	24	28	AC	80	ABCDE
Sarah	11	1993	10	05	ADE	10	ABCE
Mr Clem	t	1988	35	10	AB	25	ACE

2. When you finish your database, analyse it. One way to help you to do this is by making a graph. This could be a pie graph or bar chart. For example: Make a graph that shows what is the most common reason people give for starting to smoke? Or, what is the most common effect on health?

F. Help sheet for chapter five of smoking booklet: Drawing Conclusions

Use evidence from Chapters 2, 3 and 4 to discuss the research question, 'Does smoking affect your health?' to back up all the conclusions you make. Provide reasons for your opinions.

G. Help sheet for writing and completing your smoking booklet

Helpful hints for the booklet

Make an attractive cover. Design it on a piece of scratch paper or create a design on computer with a graphics programme.

Use Encarta, SIRS, Facts on File and the Readers' Guide to Periodical Literature rather than books to collect current information.

Find a graphics programme to draw the experimental set-up of the smoking machine.

Use the help sheets in your packet for each chapter of your booklet.

Chapter 1 Checklist:

Write a title.

Write one page about the history of smoking using your notes.

Chapter 2 Checklist:

Write a title.

Type an introductory statement.

Insert diagram of smoking machine showing where the various poisons accumulate.

Choose five of the poisons and write several sentences about each describing something about them such as how they poison the body.

Chapter 3 Checklist:

Write your questionnaire.

Gather data.

Write a title for the chapter.

Type an introductory sentence. Example: 'I wanted to find out...'

Type the questionnaire without the data.

On computer ask a question. Example: 'What percentage of people in school smoke?

Print out a graph.

Type in a conclusion. Example: 49% of people in school smoke.

Ask another question. Example: I wonder what percentage of the 49% who smoke are teachers and what percentage are students. Bring this question to your Maths class for discussion and group work on the problems.

Type four or five paragraphs to describe the diseases caused by smoking.

Illustrate with coloured drawings.

Chapter 4 Checklist:

Create a title.

Summarize the latest research on smoking. Include statistics.

Chapter 5 Checklist:

Create a title.

Answer the questions, Will you (continue) to smoke? Will you ever try smoking? What will you do if all your friends want you to smoke?

List reasons for not starting to smoke.

Finish the project with a concluding statement about what you think about smoking.

H. Library packet

SMOKING PROJECT:

Does smoking affect your health?

Name _____

Section _____

H1. Where do I look in the library for information?

The sources of information and resources found in the library that will be most helpful for gathering information and data are listed below. Locate them and use the HELP poster at each of these workstations. Even if you have used programs such as the library catalogue or *Encarta on CD-ROM*, use the HELP poster to learn about a feature or option you have never used before.

Library catalogue
Go to the key word search screen and enter your search words.

Encarta on CD-ROM

General Encyclopaedias

SIRS
Use Subject Search (Full-text articles and F2)
Use Key Word Search

Facts on File
Access through Library Catalogue using F10

Folders located at the Circulation Desk labelled 'Smoking Trends and Statistics'

Reserve shelf
Place all books, magazines, and articles from the folders
on the Reserve Cart labelled 'Smoking Project – [name of teacher]'

H2. Timeline of the history of smoking

Directions: Place the dates and the important facts about the events in the history of smoking on the timeline. You must have at least four dates and events on your timeline. You will use these notes to write Chapter 1 of your brochure.

Dates
Events

H3. Table of statistics

Directions:

Label the categories for the statistics you are collecting in the table below. You should have the name, or category, at the top of the column with the numbers under it. The information you need can be found on the reserve shelf or at the circulation desk. You will use these statistics for your spreadsheet.

H4. Bibliography chart

Bibliography charts are graphic organisers that help students to document their sources. It is helpful if various charts are designed to accommodate various formats of resources (*ie*, books, periodicals, web sites) and that the components (title, author, copyright) are arranged in the order in which they would appear in the reference list or bibliography. It is helpful when the librarian and teachers choose a style manual (APA, MLA, Turabian, Chicago Manual of Style) as the official school manual. A consistent, school-wide approach provides opportunities for using bibliography charts and style sheets which are abridged, simplified versions of the style manual adopted school-wide.

Bibliography chart for periodicals

Author	Date of Pub.	Title of Article	Name of Journal	Volume No Page No(s)
Example: Posner, M	1993, October 29	Seeing the mind	Science	262, 673-674

Example of a citation for writing a formal bibliography or list of references:

Posner, M (1993, October 29), Seeing the mind, *Science*, 262, 673-674.

Note: Students in grades 9-12 can use the bibliography chart to write a formal reference list or bibliography.

Recommended web sites

Rubrics

Empowering Students through Negotiable Contracting to Draft Rubrics for Authentic Assessment
http://www.interactiveclassroom.com/neg-cont.html

Kathy Schrock's Guide for Educators – Assessment Rubrics
http://school.discovery.com/schrockguide/assess.html

'Kid Language' Writing Rubrics
http://www.intercom.net/local/school/sdms/mspap/kidwrit.html

Smoking

The Teenager's Guide to the Real World. For Teenagers: Understanding Smoking – Includes a link to Great Articles for Teenagers and discussion of why teens smoke.
http://www.bygpub.com/books/tg2rw/smoking.htm

Chapter Six

Top Secret: A Search and Detect Mission of Analysis

Activity:	Top Secret
Level:	Grades 5-9
Interdisciplinary Action:	Social Studies/humanities; English/language arts
Information Literacy Focus:	Display and analysis of information
Project Designer:	Sue Corlett, Frankfurt International School

Project description

This project involves an investigation into the development of countries in Eastern and Western Europe. Each student assumes the identity of a government agent who is sent on a mission by Headquarters to uncover geographical, historical and economic data that have aided or hindered the country's development in the last 150 years. The teacher, who assumes the identity of Special Agent at HQ, poses the research question that guides this mission. A country is assigned to each student from a list of developing countries.

The following research skills are necessary for completing the 'mission':

Data collection: Students gather data from variety of sources: reference books, electronic sources, encyclopaedias, periodicals, using note taking sheets found in the student packet to record data. A bibliography is assembled in note-taking form and transferred to a standard APA style sheet.

Data application: Students apply the data, creating graphs and charts to help them to develop a sense of this country's placement on the developmental scale.

Data correlation: Students correlate the data, writing paragraphs, including an introduction, which pull together the facts and present them in a cohesive manner.

Data summation and evaluation: Based on notes, graphs and correlated data, students analyse the data and write a conclusion, summing up all data and answering the research question, 'How have the history, geography and industry (economy) of the country affected its overall development?' Students make recommendations in a written report to HQ regarding the prospect of investing in the developing countries based on the evidence they have collected. Students make predictions regarding the direction the country will take in the future based on collected data, notes and graphs. Students write reports for Headquarters, from the point of view of a young person in the country they are investigating. They use and apply data gathered to describe such things as life-style, food, holidays, jobs and school.

All completed research packets, including notes, data, graphs, summations, evaluations, essay and bibliography are handed in and graded by the English and humanities/social studies teachers.

Support materials (p117-134)

A. Student packet

1. Preparing for the mission – pre-mission task, day 1

2. Preparing for the mission – classified material for East and West European mission, day 2

3. Preparing for the mission – mission dossier, day 3

4. Preparing for the mission – top secret coded message for access to information sources at the library of top secret documents, day 4

5. Mission one: uncovering geographical information, day 5

6. Mission one: uncovering geographical information – geographic summary report, day 6

7. Mission one: uncovering geographical information, day 7

8. Mission two: uncovering the past, day 8

9. Mission two: uncovering the past, day 9

10. Mission two: uncovering the past, day 10

11. Mission three: finding the figures, day 11

12. Mission three: classified material for drawing conclusions, day 12

13. Mission three: economic summary, day 13

14. The final mission: top secret report, day 14

15. Bibliography charts

Evaluation of student achievement

EAST WEST TOP SECRET REPORT

Ratings	Standards
GEOGRAPHICAL REPORT	
10-7	Agents can describe the main physical and climate regions of the country and give examples. Agents will also make sound assessments of the importance of each in development based on research materials.
6-3	Agents can describe the main physical and climate regions with some examples. Agents will have assigned the rank based on some of the researched material.
2-0	Agents give only vague descriptions of physical or climatic regions. The ranking of importance has been completed but there is no support from researched material.
TIME LINE	
10-7	Agents show clearly 10 events that have had an impact on the country's economic development. Agents use an appropriate scale and clear labels. Agents have given appropriate scores for importance based on their research.
6-3	Agents show 10 events with little impact on economic development. The scale is appropriate but not all the labels are clear. Agents have given appropriate scores and given limited reference to their research.
2-0	Agents give events with no impact on economic development. The scale and labelling are not clear. Agents have given scores to the events.
STATISTICS CHART	
10-7	Agents complete the statistics chart with all the figures in the correct unit of measurement.
6-3	Agents complete the statistics chart with all the figures but not in the correct measurement.
2-0	Agents do not complete the chart.
GRAPHS	
10-7	Appropriate statistics are chosen and presented with titles, labels, keys, scales, accuracy and a sentence describing what the graph shows.
6-3	Inappropriate choices and graphs are used. Some inaccuracies and the descriptions of what the graph shows are not comprehensive. Titles, labels, keys and scales are included.
2-0	Inappropriate choices and graphs are drawn inaccurately and do not include titles, labels, keys and scales.
TOP SECRET REPORT	
10-7	Agents make clear links with the history, geography and statistics to describe the position of the country on the scale of development and make recommendations for future aid based upon this summary.
6-3	Agents link the history, geography and statistics to the position of the country on the development scale and make recommendations partially based on this summary.
2-0	Agents report the geography, history and statistical information but do not draw clear conclusions from it and the recommendations are not clearly linked to this summary.
FUTURE PROJECTS	
10-7	Agents present a logical plan based on their findings in the report. It relates closely to the needs of the country. The recommendations have valid reasons linked to the needs of the country.
6-3	Agents present a clear plan, which is clearly based on the findings of the report. The recommendation and reasons do not relate to the needs of the country.
2-0	Agents present a plan with no relationship to their findings and the recommendations do not relate to the needs of the country.

RESEARCH SKILLS	
10-7	Agents understand and can use the library, use a variety of sources, and different types (secondary and primary). Bibliography Charts are completed. Agents have spent full 15-minutes using electronic resources. Overt Operations Chief [librarian's name] will verify this requirement by initialling student visas.
6-3	Agents can use the library but use limited sources and secondary notes. Some sources on the Bibliography Chart and notes are incomplete or unclear. Agents have spent full 15-minutes using electronic resources. Overt Operations Chief [librarian's name] will verify this requirement by initialling student visas.
2-0	Agents use the library very little and only one source type (eg almanac). Sources are not noted on Bibliography Chart and notes are missing and unclear. Agents have spent some time using electronic resources. Overt Operations Chief [librarians name] will verify this requirement by initialling student visas.

Reflection
The role of display in analysis

Analysis is a critical thinking skill that is inherent in the concept of doing research. Students consistently rate it as the most difficult requirement of information handling. The quantity and complexity of text often confuse the young researcher who is struggling to sort out what is relevant and 'what the teacher wants'. (Refer to Chapter Four: *Emergency Rescue Package* for a discussion of reading strategies.) Graphics and displays are useful to keep students focused and to help them analyse the materials they have collected.

Computer generated displays such as charts and graphs, as shown in *Top Secret*, help students to focus on data that is relevant to the research question. The display is not an end in itself: it must be accompanied by oral or written analysis. The following kinds of data display are most useful when accompanied by examples of the displays as well as examples of analytical text that is drawn from the displays.

1. Tables display information or data. They contain words or numbers, and the columns and rows are labelled. The writer refers to the information in the table, looking for patterns or important trends. This information becomes evidence in the analysis. If the table contains information the researcher collected from primary sources (interviews, questionnaires) citation is not necessary; if it is copied from a published source, it must be cited. The table

113

should appear on the same page as the reference(s) to it in the text.

Example 1
Table 1: Mean numbers of words as a function of interstimulus interval

Interstimulus Intervals

Subject	25	50	75	100
1	2.6	3.0	2.6	3.0
2	2.8	1.8	2.0	3.0
3	1.6	2.2	2.8	3.0

2. Figures are data represented by graphs, photographs, mind maps, diagrams, drawings, graphic organisers. A model, or graphic representation of a process to illustrate how something happens. Models are mind maps that show the connections among data and/or information. A source footnote should appear on the same page as the reference to it in your text. A source footnote for figures copied from published works would contain the same bibliographic information as the bibliography or reference list.

Figure 1 below illustrates how the drawings of children who were interviewed in a study of displaced children are placed in the research paper. The actual drawings are used as evidence to explore the emotional characteristics of the children. The text of the research paper analyses the drawings, referring to Figure 1 in the process. It may be significant; for example, that the tree is bare and the season depicted is winter. Note the source footnote at the bottom of the figure.

Example 2
Figure 1: Drawings by displaced children

From Smith, Rosalie, 'Stimulus Deprivation and Creative Expression in Children'. *Journal of Experimental Psychology: Human Perception and Performance* 13.3-4 (1991): 611.

Figure 2 is an example from a research paper on child abuse. It shows how a student interpreted the cycle of child abuse in a diagram. This is called a model: the student found characteristics that were common to all the cases of child abuse that she studied and drew a model that illustrated these characteristics. The text of the research paper explains the model, referring to Figure 2.

Example 3
Figure 2: The cycle of child abuse

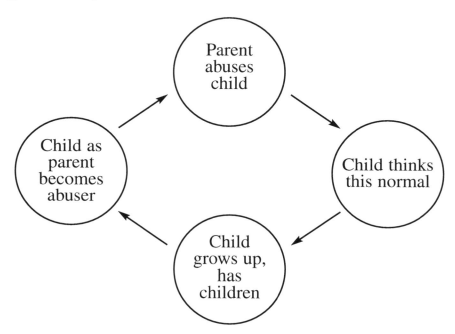

Kuhlthau's Model of the Search Process, found in Chapter 7 (page 148) can also be used as an example and has the added benefit of helping students understand their emotional and cognitive transitions during the research process.

3. Quotations or paraphrasing accompanied by citations are the exact words or re-wordings or someone else's writing and should not exceed 10% of the total word limit of the essay or paper.

Students do not think of quotations as data display because they see the quotation as text rather than a graphic. They often have difficulty seeing text as an illustrative tool to expand on a point, provide an example, present evidence, or summarise an idea or theory. Using quotation effectively often emerges as the most poorly executed display option in students' research papers. Students lack experience with citation, or find the text dense and indecipherable. They often equate the mechanics of citation, *ie* correct format for a footnote or endnote, with the use of quotation as an aid to analysis.

A helpful support for citation is a style sheet developed by the librarian, which abridges the style adopted by the school. If, for example, the English department adopts APA or MLA style, the librarian can supply style sheets that summarise the rules used most often for citation and provide contextual examples of what the citations looks like. The style sheets can be compiled in booklets for older students who are engaged in a sustained research project and should be made available in the library. Bibliographies or Reference Lists an also be covered in style sheets. The style sheet is an appropriate vehicle for defining and discussing plagiarism and Internet use and the consequences of infractions with regard to school policy.

When analysis degenerates to opinion or plagiarised conclusions in students' research papers it is usually because students are not aware of the variety of analytical methods and have not had opportunities to practise them. It is not surprising that compare/contrast, pros/cons, chronological order and cause/effect are overworked. Seldom do students apply structural analysis, a thematic approach, classification, or problem/solution methods. Furthermore, they often do not see the connection between the academic discipline from which their research question grows and the appropriate form of analysis for that discipline. It is helpful if students learn the difference between qualitative and quantitative research and their attendant methods so that they can make conscious choices about data collection and analysis based on the academic discipline and the nature of their research questions. See Chapter 7 for support materials that outline various methods of analysis.

Children can exercise analytical skills through the use of illustrations. A picture can elicit a thousand words of dialogue as details and contextual clues lead to analytical talk. The web site such as *The Amazing Picture Machine* includes a search screen and a wide variety of pictures. **http://www.ncrtec.org/picture.htm**

Support Materials
for Chapter Six

Activity: Top Secret
Information Literacy Focus: Display and analysis of
                                       information

A. Student packet – cover page

TOP SECRET MISSION

Photo ID

AGENT _____

IDENTIFICATION NO _____

Date of Entry	Customs Stamp
	[school acronym] Library

Visa: This visa is valid for five visits to the library. Visa approval is contingent upon meeting work deadlines.

A1: Preparing for the mission

Day 1

Pre mission task

Before you go on your mission to the assigned country you must be prepared.

Read the data researched by MI25 on your country's climate, physical background and major products.

Using this list put together a packing list of 10 items you will need on this journey.

PACKING LIST

1.

2.

3.

4.

5.

6.

7.

8.

9.

10.

Be prepared to justify your packing list to the special agent in charge of this pre mission task.

See Agent [name of librarian] if you need a visa to enter the Library of Top Secret Documents.

A2: Preparing for the mission

Day 2

Classified material for East and West European mission

PERSONAL DATA:
Name: Gender:
Nationality:

THE MISSION:
To investigate physical geography and history, assess the economy of
_____, a developing European nation.

TRAVEL INFORMATION:
You will travel on the wings of research booked, interviews and stories to gather information on your country. Your imagination will transport you there as will your love of creative writing, journal writing and drawing.

Departure	Return
8 May 2001 at 08:40	5 June 2001 at 14:55
Flight #AO!9	Flight # AO!10
Super Economy Class	Super Economy Class
Stop: Amsterdam	Stop: Brussels
Destination:	Destination: Frankfurt
Airline: Imaginaire	Airline: Imaginaire

FINAL OBJECTIVE:
A formal report in which you will assess your country on a development scale of 1 to 6, where 6 is highly developed and 1 is less developed, in terms of economic affluence and standard of living. The report will contain:

- Confidential memos on the geography, history and economics, and graphs gathered and prepared through research and primary sources.
- An 'Espionage Dossier' containing a journal of your successes and failures on the mission. (You will need a notebook for this.)
- A formal letter to HQ making recommendations on the top-secret assignment.
- Completed 'Special Alert' sheet assessing the risk of infiltration by other agents.
- For services above and beyond the call of an agent's duty, which gives an agent extra credit, follow this directive: Arrange a meeting place with Special Agent [name of teacher]. Include: a description of a meeting place and a menu for a typical meal.

FINAL REPORTS TO BE HANDED TO SPECIAL AGENTS [name of teacher] AND [name of teacher] ON [date].

A3: Preparing for the mission

Day 3

Mission dossier

You need to keep a journal record of your successes and failures on this mission.

This journal will form a mission dossier which HQ may decide to use for the training of future spies.

Here are your instructions:

Purchase an A5 notebook. Keep this somewhere safe at all times.
Do not let this fall into another agent's hands.
Keep a record in your journal of your achievements on the mission.

Here are some ideas for writing:

What have you achieved at each stage of the mission?

What have you found difficult and why?

What have you found particularly interesting?

How did you solve problems you encountered?

What contributions did you make to solving team problems?

What codes did you manage to crack?

What support did you give to other agents?

Special Agent [name of teacher], who is in charge of report writing, will provide further guidance on this top secret dossier.
The Dossier should be given to Special Agent [name of teacher] at the end of the mission, on [date].

A4: Preparing for the mission

Day 4

Top-secret coded message for access to information sources at the library of top secret documents

Code 1.   LC+F7=940.0-959
             LC+F8=940.0-959

Code 2.   LC+F10=FOF

Code 3.   CD-ROMs
             Global Explorer
             CIA
             Grolier
             Electronic VF

Code 4.   Highly Confidential VF

Code 5.   TOP-SECRET HIGHLY CONFIDENTIAL AUTHORIZED
             PERSONNEL ONLY RESERVE CART

Code 6.   TOP SECRET DOCUMENTS

REF 330 ECO	The Economist Atlas and Almanac
REF 310.9 TRE	Trends in Developing Economies
REF 310 WOR	World Tables
REF LAN	Lands and People
REF 031	General Encyclopaedias
REF 317 WOR	World Almanac and Book of Facts
REF 310.5	Statesman's Yearbook
REF 310 STA	Statistical Yearbook
914 WOO	Cheap Eats
REF 947 RUS	Russia, The Eurasian Republics and Central/Eastern Europe
REF 909	History of the World
REF 912 WOR	World Reference Atlas; The Commonwealth Of Independent States
REF 910.3 WEB	Webster's Geographical Dictionary

AGENTS: TAKE NOTE
There are documents that have not yet been retrieved. Use Code 1 to find these documents and place them on the top-secret reserve cart.

A5: Mission one: uncovering geographical information

Day 5

Confidential memo one

When you arrive in your country you must write a report on the geography of the country so that other agents who follow are prepared. To help, Special Agent [name of teacher] has prepared this paper as a guide for information collection. Do not let it fall into enemy hands.

Geographical data checklist
Major land forms
Major water forms
Climate(s)
Industries

A6: Mission one: uncovering geographical information

Day 6

Geographic summary report

List geographic features that helped and prevented development. Assign a percentage ranking to each according to its importance.

Example:

Overpopulation	50%
Desert	30%
Drought	20%
Total	100%

Make a pie chart of geographic factors.

Example:

Geographical summary

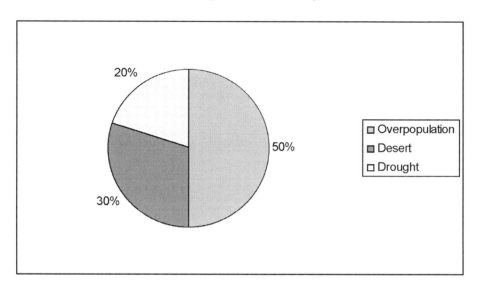

A7: Mission one: uncovering geographical information

Day 7

Model for geography section of your report

_____has many/few physical regions. The major features are _____

_____ These have helped/stopped development because _____

_____

_____has many/few water forms. The major features are _____

_____These have helped/stopped development because _____

_____

_____

The climate of _____ is _____

_____

_____. This has helped/stopped development because

_____

_____

_____

The main industries are _____

_____

_____

_____These are large and complex and provide a large income for the country/these are small and simple and provide limited income for the country.

A 8: Mission two

Day 8

Uncovering the past

If you have reached this stage safely, well done Agent. Now to prepare for what may happen, we must be aware of what has happened in the past.

Find 10 historical events, which may have affected your country's development. Use the last 150 years.
Special Agent [name of teacher] has provided a memo sheet to help you.

Historical Data	Date
1.	
2.	
3.	
4.	
5.	
6.	
7.	
8.	
9.	
10.	

A9: Mission two: uncovering the past

Day 9

Top-secret time line

Agents need to draw a time line using the ten events they have researched.

Include:

- a correct scale

- a clear title

- well-written labels.

A10: Mission two: uncovering the past

Day 10

Historical summary report

List the ten most important events in the country's history.

Give a value of + or -1 for each event. The events labelled + are those that had a positive impact on development. The events labelled - are those that had a negative effects on development. The number you choose reflects the importance of the event, with +10 being the most important and -10 being the least important.

For example:

Granted independence in 1988	+ 8
Discovery of copper in 1960	+10
Military coup in 1962	-10
Race riots in 1959	-7

Plot the events on a bar graph.

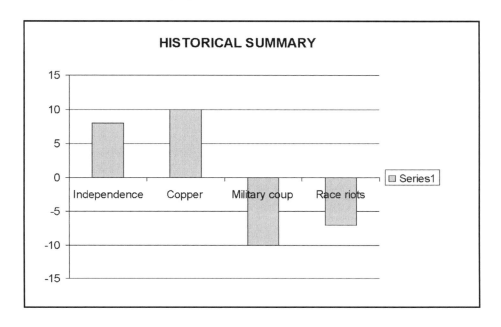

 # A11: Mission three: finding the figures

Day 11

Confidential memo

East West Mission

Mission 3

You are now on a search and detect mission.

You must find out how developed the country you are visiting is in economic terms.

This information is vital to determine what future links and development will be available to this country.

Complete the statistical chart given.

When you have completed your research decide on an appropriate form for presenting your findings to Headquarters.

A12: Mission three: classified material for drawing conclusions

Day 12

Use the special coded material to complete this table.

Development Scale	1	2	3	4	5	6	Yours
Life expectancy in years	65	70	67	78	75	78.5	
Birth rate per 1000 people	35	16	12	13	15	11	
Death rate per 1000 people	8	10	14	13	9	12	
Adult literacy %	89	98	98	99	99	99	
Urban/Rural pop.%	52/48	60/40	60/40	77/23	76/24	86/14	
GNP per head in US$	NA	1930	2240	9800	18350	14400	
People per TVs	18	3.8	2.5	2.7	1.3	2.5	
Newspaper circ Per 1000 people	91	217	236	559	255	417	
People per telephone	31	5.0	6.6	5.0	1.3	1.7	

A13: Mission three: economic summary

Day 13

Use the ratings on your Statistics Chart to make a bar graph.

Example:

Life expectancy	4
Birth rate	7
Death rate	6
Adult literacy	5
Avg annual per capita income	4
Urban/rural population	4
GNP	5
People per TVs	3
No of cars (mil)	3
Newspaper circ. (per 1000)	2

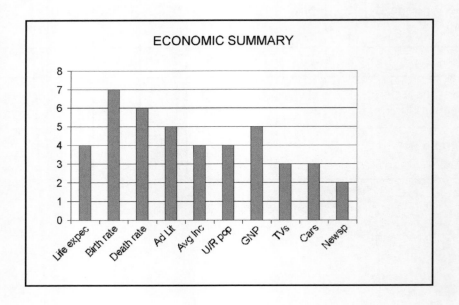

A14: THE FINAL MISSION: TOP SECRET REPORT

Day 14

Instructions:

Your mission is to use your summary reports to write a final report to Special Agent [name of teacher]. Include the following:

1. Summarise your findings in a confidential report to Agent [name of teacher], indicating which factors (geographical, historical, economic) most affected the development status of the country you are investigating. Discuss whether these factors affected one another.
2. The potential investors listed in the chart below are interested in providing venture capital for developing European nations. Make your recommendation to support or not support investment by each potential investor, in the country you have investigated. **Provide a geographical, historical or economic reason from your confidential memo for each recommendation.**

Potential Investors	YES	NO	REASON
1. Travel on a Shoestring			
2. Ring-a-ding Communications			
3. XYZ Motion Pictures			
4. Waldo Wall's Habitats			
5. Sparky Electric Company			
6. Tinkertech Computers			
7. Rapid Railroad			
8. Podunk International School			
9. MacMurphy's Hamburger Heaven			

3. Make recommendations to the country you have investigated regarding the kinds of FOREIGN AID they should request from more developed countries. Give a geographic, historical and economic reason from your confidential memo for your recommendations. Prioritise your recommendations, listing the most important first.

Recommendations	Reasons
1.	
2.	
3.	
4.	
5.	

A15. Bibliography charts

See Chapters 2 and 5 for examples of Bibliography Charts. For this unit a chart for electronic resources should be included. The headings for columns should be sequenced to correspond with the elements included in a formal citation (*eg* author if given, title of document, year or date of publication, number of pages or paragraphs, publication medium, URL or web address, date of access.).

Recommended web sites
Analysis and other thinking skills

The following sites provide ideas for activities to elicit thinking on the knowledge, comprehension, and higher levels of thinking described in Bloom's Taxonomy.

http://www.it.utk.edu/~jklittle/edsmrt521/cognitive.html

http://ils.unc.edu/daniel/242/Bloom.html

http://www.ais.msstate.edu/TALS/unit1/1moduleB.html

http://www.umcs.maine.edu/~orono/collaborative/spring/appC.html

http://www.coun.uvic.ca/learn/program/hndouts/bloom.html

The Amazing Picture Machine
http://www.ncrtec.org/picture.htm

Social Studies/Humanities
CIA-The World Factbook 1999
http://www.odci.gov/cia/publications/factbook/index.html

Euro Data Map – a resource for economic data.
http://www.washingtonpost.com/wp-srv/inatl/longterm/euro/euromap.htm

Kid's Almanac
http://www.factmonster.com

US State Department – services background notes
http://www.state.gov/www/background_notes/index.html

Chapter Seven

Students as Authentic Researchers: Upgrading the Research Paper

Activity:	The 10th Grade Research Paper
Level:	Grades 10-12
Interdisciplinary Action:	All subjects
Information Literacy Focus:	Establishing focus, gathering data, analysing data
Project Designer:	Carol Gordon

Project description

Does 'doing research' have to be limited to highlighting photocopied text from books and magazine articles and printing out from Internet sites or CD-ROMs? Can the research paper assignment be adapted to promote creative thinking and problem solving? Can students successfully use primary research methods to collect their own data? What if research assignments distinguished between information and data *ie*, between other people's answers recorded in books and electronic sources, and evidence, or data, collected first-hand by the student researcher? This chapter addresses the distinction between 'reporting' and 'researching'. (See 'Reflection: Reporting *v* Researching' in Chapter 5.) Support Materials target three information literacy skill areas: 1) focus and the research question; 2) data collection; and 3) data analysis.

Students received instruction and support from the librarian during a class that met once a week when this unit was first implemented. The second year the project was placed in the English curriculum and teachers collaborated with the librarian to provide instruction and support. Students learned about the Kuhlthau model to develop an appreciation for the concept of 'focus'. Class discussion included the emotional and cognitive stages presented in the model. Topic choice was deferred until students had spent three days engaged in background reading in the library. Note taking was prohibited at this stage. When they had acquired or supplemented their knowledge of a topic and assessed the availability of resources, students wrote Proposal One. Only after approval of this proposal by the teacher or librarian did students proceed to note taking. Students who were having difficulty focusing and formulating a research question received individual help.

The second stage, data collection, included distinguishing between quantitative and qualitative research and designing and administering questionnaires, interviews or experiments that were appropriate to the research question. (The questionnaire developed by teachers and the librarian and administered at the end of this unit as part of the action research component was used as an example of a data collection instrument.) Help sheets presented in a checklist format outlined how to design these instruments. The third stage, data analysis, included a variety of analytical methods and the concept of display. Displays were defined as models (such as the Kuhlthau model), figures (*eg*, charts diagrams, photos, sketches) and tables. These displays helped students to look at the data and analyse it in a paragraph that accompanied the display. At least one original display and two citations were required to facilitate analysis in the text of the research paper. (See Chapter 6, *Reflections: The Role of Display in Analysis*.)

The outcome of the project was an essay of 2000 words with a formal bibliography. The English teachers used the writing process, including peer review of rough drafts. Students were required to include an Appendix to their final papers, with support materials such as Proposal One and Two, notes and bibliography charts included. The Appendix received 50% of the entire grade for the research paper. The librarian shared the results of the questionnaires that students completed at the end of the unit and discussed proposed changes in the unit with them. Data from the questionnaire, teachers' observations that were noted throughout the unit, and a post-mortem meeting of teachers with the librarian, provided data for the action research study aimed at modification of the unit for next year.

Support materials (p148-168)

A Kuhlthau Model of the search process

B Example of proposal one

C Example of proposal two

D How to write a proposal

E Choosing a data collection method: quantitative and qualitative research – What's the difference?

F Primary research instruments

    F1 How to do a questionnaire or survey

    F2 How to do an interview

    F3 How to do a respondent profile

    F4 How to do a letter of informed consent

G How do I analyse data?

    G1 Methods of analysis

    G2 Asking analytical questions

H Project evaluation of the 10th grade research paper

Evaluation of student achievement

A. Peer editing of rough draft: PQP

Directions:

Use your checklist of requirements and the assessment criteria to edit a classmate's rough draft. Do not discuss your papers with each other until you have finished peer editing.

INCLUDE THE PQP FORM DONE FOR YOUR PAPER IN THE APPENDIX.

PRAISE (What are the strengths of the paper? Be specific: refer to the checklist and descriptors.)
QUESTIONS (What would you like to ask the writer to make the paper clearer, more complete, or better written?)
POLISH (What suggestions do you have to improve the paper regarding its content, format and written style?)

Edited for: _____ Edited by: _____

B. The appendix of the research paper: checklist

The librarian will grade the Appendix of your paper for completeness using the checklist found below and a point system. All of the following items, in completed form, are required for credit. No partial credit is given. The Appendix comprises 50% of the total grade for the research paper.

	Proposal One	10 points
	Proposal Two	10 points
	Notes	10 points
	Bibliography charts	5 points
	Rough draft of paper	5 points
	PQP peer editing form	5 points
	Assessment criteria (Rubric) for research management (Self-evaluation)	5 points
	TOTAL	50 points

Your research paper will be graded by your teacher, using the assessment criteria (Rubric) for the research paper - 50 points

Signed by: _____
Librarian

C. Assessment criteria (Rubric) for research management (self-assessment)

NAME _____

TOPIC _____

EXCELLENT – 4

PERSONAL ENGAGEMENT	MANAGING TIME	RESEARCH PROPOSAL	NOTES AND DATA	RESOURCES
Student liked the topic and felt motivated to learn about it. Student was curious and/or enthusiastic about the research question. Student took responsibility for his/her own learning by taking the initiative to get things done. Student sought advice when needed from teachers and/or peers. Student spent time outside the school-day thinking about the project when not reading or writing about it. Student formed several opinions, judgements and/or had reactions or questions to readings and discoveries.	Proposal 1 and 2 submitted on time. Adequate notes presented for both note checks. Rough Draft ready on time. Paper handed in on time.	Proposal 1 includes research question, at least two sub-questions, at least four key words and three resources in working bibliography. Proposal 2 includes one data collection method fully appropriate to the type of research done and one fully appropriate method of analysis. Proposal 1 & 2 approved.	Notes in at least four sources are thorough, relevant and efficient. Notes used to develop the topic and address the research question. Four direct/indirect quotations included and keyed to sources (cited). Data generated from a primary source and recorded in a thorough and careful manner.	At least four sources of information appear in bibliography. Sources are authoritative and/or accurate. Sources are relevant to the topic and research question. Sources are objective, or there is a balance of points of view or bias is declared and/or analysed by the writer. Sources are up-to-date for contemporary issues or topics that are of contemporary significance.

Evidence:
Give examples from the paper or a reference with page and line number

COMPETENT – 3

PERSONAL ENGAGEMENT	MANAGING TIME	RESEARCH PROPOSAL	NOTES AND DATA	RESOURCES
Student liked the topic and felt motivated to learn about it. Student was interested in the research question. Student took responsibility for his/her own learning and initiated research tasks most of the time. Student occasionally sought advice when needed from teachers and/or peers. Student occasionally spent time outside the school-day thinking about the project when not reading or writing about it. Student formed a few opinions, judgements and/or had reactions or questions to readings and discoveries.	All items, with one exception, ready and on time.	Proposal 1 includes the research question, one sub-question, 2-3 key words and 2-3 resources in working bibliography. Proposal 2 includes one appropriate data collection method and one method of analysis. Proposal 1 & 2 approved.	Notes are adequate and related, for the most part, to the topic and mostly efficient. Notes used to develop the topic and address the research question. Four direct/indirect quotations included and keyed to sources (cited). Data generated from a primary source and adequately recorded.	Two to three sources of information appear in bibliography. The paper refers to the sources. Sources are mostly authoritative and accurate. Sources are mostly relevant to the topic and research question. Sources are objective, or there is a balance of points of view. If relevant, sources are up-to-date.

Evidence:
Give examples from the paper or a reference with page and line number

BARELY ADEQUATE – 2

PERSONAL ENGAGEMENT	MANAGING TIME	RESEARCH PROPOSAL	NOTES AND DATA	RESOURCES
Student settled for the topic and learned about the topic because it was a school requirement.	All items, with two exceptions, ready and on time.	Proposal 1 missing one sub-question, 2-3 key words and 2-3 resources in working bibliography.	Notes are either wordy or skimpy, and often not relevant to the topic or research question.	One source of information appears in bibliography.
Student was somewhat interested in the research question.		Proposal 2 missing one data collection method and/or one method of analysis, methods were not appropriate to the type of research done.	Most of the notes not used to develop the topic and address the research question.	The paper does not refer to the sources.
Student needed adult supervision in order to take responsibility for his/her own learning.			One direct/indirect quotation included and keyed to sources (cited).	Some sources are not authoritative and/or accurate.
Student did not seek advice when needed from teachers and/or peers.			Data generated from a primary source and carelessly recorded.	Some sources are not relevant to the topic and research question.
Student spent little time outside the school-day thinking about the project when not reading or writing about it.				Some sources are not objective, or there is not a balance of points of view.
Student formed a few opinions, judgements and/or had reactions or questions to readings and discoveries.				If relevant, some sources are not up-to-date.

Evidence:
Give examples from the paper or a reference with page and line number

142

NOT YET COMPETENT – 1

PERSONAL ENGAGEMENT	MANAGING TIME	RESEARCH PROPOSAL	NOTES AND DATA	RESOURCES
Student disliked the topic and had no motivation to learn about it. Student was uninterested or apathetic about the research question. Student did not take responsibility for learning even with assistance. Student did not seek advice when needed from teachers and/or peers. Student spent no time outside the school-day thinking about the project when not reading or writing about it. Student formed no opinions, judgements and/or had no reactions or questions to readings and discoveries.	Three or more deadlines missed.	Proposal 1 missing the research question and/or one sub-question, key words and/or resources in working bibliography. Proposal 2 missing one data collection method and/or one method of analysis and/or methods were not appropriate to the type of research done.	Notes are sketchy and often not relevant to the topic or research question and/or plagiarised (not cited when word-for-word). Notes not used to develop the topic and address the research question. Direct/indirect quotations missing. Little or no data generated from a primary source.	Bibliography is missing or contains one source. Sources are not authoritative and/or accurate. Some sources are not relevant to the topic and research question. Some sources are not objective, or there is not a balance of points of view. If relevant, some sources are not up-to-date.

Evidence:
Give examples from the paper or a reference with page and line number

143

D. Assessment criteria (Rubric) for the research paper

	BUILDING YOUR ARGUMENT			
	INTRODUCTION	MAIN ANALYSIS	SUPPORTING EVIDENCE	CONCLUSION
4	Reader's interest skilfully raised; research question both sharply focused and clearly stated; terms and scope of essay precisely defined; if appropriate, thesis clearly stated.	Precise, persuasive, highly relevant key argument points, completely covering research question, using at least two analysis methods, showing independence of thought and awareness of more than one viewpoint.	Points are all supported with a variety of relevant, accurate and convincing evidence, (such as facts, statistics, detailed argument); at least four quotations; at least one visual display of information (table, graph, etc); at least one source not notes from secondary material.	Forceful, fully convincing conclusion, clearly stated, which fully meets terms of initial research question, and recognises further issues raised *and/or* complications *and/or* modifications to thesis.
3	Reader's interest gained; research question both appropriate and clearly stated; terms and scope of essay defined; if appropriate, thesis stated.	Various relevant persuasive, argument points, covering main aspects of research question, using at least two analysis methods.	Points are supported with relevant, accurate and mostly convincing evidence (such as facts, statistics, detailed argument) at least four quotations; at least one visual display of information (table, graph, etc); at least one source not notes from secondary material.	Clear, suitable conclusion which meets terms of initial research question, but may fail to note important further issues raised *and/or* qualifications complications *and/or* modifications to thesis.
2	Research question stated, but too broad *and/or* terms and scope not well defined; thesis may be inadequately stated.	A few points, not always persuasive or fully relevant, *and/or* some omissions.	Most points are supported with some evidence, such as facts, statistics, quotations, detailed argument.	Conclusion stated, but only partly meets terms of initial research question, *and/or* fails to recognise important further issues raised *and/or* qualifications.
1	Research question stated confusingly *and/or* far too broad, *and/or* terms and scope not defined; *and/or* thesis, if any, inappropriate/ confused.	Claims made are (partly) irrelevant, *and/or* unpersuasive *and/or* repetitive *and/or* missing important points.	Few points are supported with evidence, *and/or* evidence is irrelevant/inaccurate/ unconvincing.	No conclusion, or very weak/inappropriate conclusion *and/or* confusingly stated, *and/or* doesn't meet terms of initial research question, *and/or* fails to recognise important further issues raised *and/or* qualifications.

WRITING THE ESSAY – FORMAL ASPECTS			
ORGANISATION	USE OF LANGUAGE	REFERENCING & LAYOUT	MECHANICS
4 Material suitably divided in paragraphs; paragraphs logically sequenced; paragraphs have topic sentences; paragraphs are linked with transitions.	Fully appropriate register; precise and concise expression; varied sentence structure with some complexity; distinctive turns of phrase; sense of individual 'voice'.		
3 Material suitably divided in paragraphs; paragraphs on the whole logically sequenced; paragraphs have topic sentences; most paragraphs are linked with transitions.	Appropriate register; effective expression; varied sentence structures.	Thoroughly complete, appropriate citations and bibliography (at least four sources used), using a consistent referencing system (see school's Style Guide); cover page; contents page; page numbering; overall layout; number of words used stated.	Very few or no errors/faults in spelling, punctuation, typing/legible handwriting.
2 Material mostly suitably divided in paragraphs; some logical sequence; most paragraphs have topic sentences; weak linking between paragraphs.	Largely appropriate register; some effective expression; some sentence variety.	Largely complete, appropriate citations, bibliography, cover page, contents page, overall layout; and statement of number of words used.	Some errors/faults in spelling, punctuation, typing/legible handwriting.
1 Poor paragraph division and/or confusing/ illogical sequence and/or few/no paragraphs with topic sentences.	Inappropriate register and/or inappropriate wording and/or little sentence variety.	Citations, bibliography, cover page, contents page, overall layout, number of words used only partially/ inaccurately/ inappropriately provided.	Several/many errors/faults in spelling, punctuation, typing/legible handwriting, impeding easy flow of reading.

Reflection
Setting a good example – the power of action research

The questionnaire administered at the end of this unit to students by teachers and the librarian was the instrument used for *action research*, so called because it takes place in the field, *ie* the school environment. This questionnaire can be adapted to any unit. Teachers also collected data by observing students and keeping notes. They brought their data to a meeting, sometimes called a post-mortem, to discuss the strengths and weaknesses of the project. The driving question behind action research is 'How can we do it better next time'.

Here is an example of the decisions that were made in an actual post-mortem session for this unit.

1. Provide focused class-time for writing. Teachers were surprised that students felt they needed more time to write and were disappointed, overall, in the quality of the writing with regard to mechanics of language. Since the peer-editing lesson was well received by students, teachers decided to provide more time for student practise with peer-editing prior to the authentic research assignment. There was consensus that more time for the Grade 10 research paper, and shorter assignments leading up to it, were needed even though this will require dropping a literature unit from the curriculum.

2. Provide more practise in using supporting evidence, including citations, in analytical thinking and drawing conclusions.

3. Use plain and direct language to reword assessment descriptors in the rubric to promote a better understanding of assessment criteria.

4. Revise citation instructions and layout of material in the school's style sheet to make it more user-friendly. It was agreed that the style sheet would be more useful in electronic format.

5. Consolidate support materials (*eg* proposal forms, bibliography charts, style sheet) into a booklet to be distributed to:
   a. students, to eliminate individual handouts and simplify organization tasks;
   b. faculty who are teaching or advising student essays.

6. Offer teachers briefing sessions, in-services, ongoing training, or more support for:

    a. Library resources and access;
    b. Research techniques for qualitative studies.

7. Offer more opportunities for students to practise information searching and expand concepts and key words and reading focused in an area of interest to prepare for the authentic research assignment by building prior knowledge of the topic.

The librarian can take a leadership role in modelling reflective practise as part of her collaboration with teachers. Planning data collection strategies when the unit is being planned, scheduling post-mortem sessions, and taking notes to be used in the planning for the next year are key initiatives to this end.

The action research study for this unit has been published in *School Library Media Research Online*, 1999, and can be found in full-text at the ECIS web site: **www.ecis.org**

References

Kuhlthau, C C (1991), Inside the search process: Information seeking from the user's perspective, *Journal of the American Society for Information Science*, 42 (5), 361-371.

Support Materials
for Chapter Seven

A. Kuhlthau model of the search process

Stages	Task Initiation	Topic Selection	Prefocus Exploration	Focus Formulation	Information Collection	Search Closure	Starting Writing
Feelings	Uncertainty	Optimism	Confusion frustration doubt	Clarity	Sense of direction confidence	Relief	Satisfaction dissatisfaction
Thoughts	Ambiguity ⟶ ⟶ specificity						
Actions	Seeking relevant information ⟶ ⟶ seeking pertinent information						

B. Example of proposal one

1. Research Question	*Sub-Questions*
Will the computer change the way we are schooled?	a. What are the positive and negative aspects of computers in learning? b. Could current problems in teaching be solved by computers? c. Will schools become obsolete?
2. Key words/terms	*Definitions of Key words/terms*
a. Information superhighway b. cognition c. virtual reality d. multimedia	a. A vast network of shared information through computer, television, and satellite. b. The act of learning and thinking. c. Computer or other electronic software that allows the user to experience a simulated environment. d. The incorporation of many types of media such as graphics, text, audio, and video into one resource.
3a.Working Bibliography: *Titles*	*3b. What do I need to find them again?* *(eg, Call number, Internet address)*
The Road Ahead The Virtual School The Children's Machine	001 GAT http:www//virtualschool.yaleuniv.edu PRO 371.3 PAP
Submitted by: _____ *Student*	Approved by: _____ _____ *Teacher* *Date*

C. Example of proposal two

4. *Research Type* Type of research for primary data collection. Check one: ✔ Qualitative (words) Quantitative (numbers)	5. *Method of Data Collection* a. Notes from secondary sources. b. Interview with a teacher. c. Questionnaires to 25 students.
6a. *Method of Analysis* Pros and cons	6b. *Why did you choose this method?* My research question will bring me to material that will point out the advantages and disadvantages of using computers in education so that I will decide how computers will change the way we learn in school in positive (pro) and negative (con) ways.
7a. *Working Bibliography: More titles* 'The Computer Revolution in Education' 'The Learning Revolution' Internet and the World Wide Web	7b. *What do I need to find them again?* (*eg*, Call number, Internet address) Time, June 28, 1996, p. 19 Educational Leadership, May 19, 1997, p. 22 001 KEN
Submitted by: _____ *Student*	Approved by: _____ _____ *Adviser/Teacher* *Date*

D. How to write a proposal

Proposal one

1. Formulate the research question and/or hypothesis. (What are you curious about? What is your informed guess that answers a 'why' or 'how' question?)

   Is the question too broad or too narrow? (Use people, places, time-frames to limit your topic.)

   Do I need a hypothesis?

   How can the question be broken down into sub-questions or sub-divisions? What are they?

2. Key Words

   Record at least four words and/or terms that are critical to your research.

   Use the key words to:
   > formulate the research question
   > search for information
   > select sources for note taking
   > take notes
   > write the essay (introduction, body, conclusion)

3. Working Bibliography

   Include the titles and location information for books, magazines, newspapers, CD- ROMs, Internet, on-line sources, people, primary sources. This is a preliminary list of sources of information that you think will be useful for note taking or that you need to read for background to help formulate your research question.

Proposal two

4. Research Type

   Choose quantitative (numerical data) or qualitative (verbal data) research.

5. Method of Data Collection

   Choose at least one method of collecting data/information using 'Quantitative and Qualitative: What's the Difference?' Explain why this is the suitable.

6. Method of Analysis

   a. Choose at least one method of analysing data/information from 'Ways to Analyse Data'.

   b. Explain why you chose this method of analysis.

7. Working Bibliography

    List other materials that will be useful as sources of information.

    Record location information for these sources.

Note: As your research progresses, elements of the proposals may change. For example, your research question may become more focused and limited to a shorter chronological time span. You may change your mind about the method of analysis as you learn more about the topic and data you are collecting. See your adviser, the librarian or your English teacher and talk with him/her about the change(s). Not all changes will be approved. Secure an initial on your proposal form, with the date of the change.

E. Choosing a data collection method
Quantitative and qualitative research – what's the difference?

Consider the following when choosing a way to collect data:

What is my topic?

What is my research question?

What kind of data can I collect (words or numbers-qualitative or quantitative?) that will provide the best evidence for my topic and research question? Use the sheet 'Qualitative and Quantitative: What is the Difference?'

Will I do qualitative or quantitative research or both? Use the sheet 'Qualitative and Quantitative: What is the Difference?'

What are my choices of data collection methods? Use the sheet 'Qualitative and Quantitative: What is the Difference?'

Which method(s) do I want to use?

Write a list of 'Things to do' to make arrangements for collecting your data.

Write a list of questions you have about the way you will collect the data (*eg* How many students should I interview?).

Data collection method	Examples of suitable subjects	Type of data	How to collect data
Note-taking (secondary sources)	All	Quantitative (numbers) Qualitative (words)	Note cards or notebook. By sources/by sub-questions/in no particular order. Photocopying, underlining, highlighting are not substitutes for note taking but can be used as a first steps. Use one side of the card or paper to help re-order your notes for the analysis stage.
Note-taking (primary sources)	History Literature Social Sciences	Quantitative (numbers) Qualitative (words)	Same as above.
Interview Set questions (closed interview) Loose categories of questions (open interview) Tape recording of interview Take notes during interview	History Psychology Social Sciences Art	Qualitative (words)	Closed Interview: bring prepared questions, leaving room between them to write responses. Open Interview: bring categories research questions and sub-questions and formulate questions from interviewee's responses. Tape record interview so you can concentrate, make eye contact, and observe body language. Transcribe (put taped responses in writing) immediately after the interview.

Data collection method	Examples of suitable subjects	Type of data	How to collect data
Questionnaire	All	Quantitative (numbers) Qualitative (words)	Prepare specific questions that address parts of the research question. Pilot (test) your questions with a few people and re-write as needed Formulate questions that will point to relationships (*eg*, male/female, age, nationality, and any other questions that may explain the interviewee's answers). Be sure your sample (number of questionnaires collected) is large enough if you are going to generalise to the entire population. Be sure your sample is a random one (*eg*, don't mail all your questionnaires to girls who are 15 years old unless that is a limitation of your study).
Participant Observation (Field work)	Social Sciences Pschology	Qualitative (words)	Arrange to be a neutral observer in a setting in which you can watch the phenomenon you are researching (*eg* how kindergarten children use their break time). Take notes and date them. Protect the identity of your subjects if necessary.
Case Study	Social Sciences Psychology History	Qualitative (words)	Choose one person, country, event that is representative of what you want to study. Use participant observation, interviews, and note taking to collect data. Protect the identity of your subject
Scientific Experiment/ Research	Mathematics Biology Chemistry Physics Geography	Quantitative (numbers)	Use the scientific method (Hypothesis testing). Keep a lab book. Choose an experiment or field study that can be done locally at home. Seek advice from a science teacher, especially if you need to use a science lab.

F. Primary research instruments

F1. How to do a questionnaire or survey
F2. How to do an interview
F3. How to do a respondent profile
F4. How to do a letter of informed consent

F1. How to do a questionnaire or survey

What is a questionnaire?

A set of questions presented to a group (usually a sample rather than the entire group).

Is a questionnaire the best way for you to collect your data?

Do you have 5-10 questions that you would like to ask 10-20 people?

Do you want to compare how answers are the same or different for sub-sets in your sample (*eg*, gender, age)?

Do you want to quantify (count) responses to look for patterns?

Do you want to analyse respondents' comments to look for patterns?

How do you do a questionnaire?

1. Select the type of sampling you will do instead of giving questionnaires to the entire population

- **Random sampling**
  Decide how many respondents you need for your sample. (Suggestion: 20% of the relevant universe.)

  Determine the relevant universe (population). For example, all high school students.

  Select a sample where all candidates have the same chance of being selected. For example, you want to survey students at FIS to determine how they feel about the ban on smoking planned for 1999. You might choose 40 people by placing the names of all FIS students in a hat and picking 40 names.

- **Stratified random sampling**
  Decide how many respondents you need for your sample. (Suggestion: 20% of the relevant universe.)

  Select a sample where you can create sub-groups with equal representation. For example, you want to survey students at FIS by grade level to see how they feel about the ban on smoking and whether there are any patterns in the data that show relationships between grade level and attitude toward the smoking ban. You might choose 10 people from each grade level at random from class grade level lists.

- **Systematic sampling**

  Decide how many respondents you need for your sample. (Suggestion: 20% of the relevant universe.)

  Make a list of the names in the population, choose one at random and count down every four or five names to choose those in the sample. For example, you want to survey all students at FIS to determine how they feel about the smoking ban. You might get a list of students, choose the second or third name as the first in the sample and count down every fourth name until you get the number of names you need in your sample.

- **Cluster sampling**

  Decide how many respondents you need for your sample. (Suggestion: 20% of the relevant universe.)

  Divide the population into small groups, or clusters and randomly sample the clusters. Include every person or household in each sample cluster. For example, to survey a city divide it into blocks, randomly sample the blocks and include every house on each sampled blocks in the survey.

2. Write the questions

Determine characteristics of your respondents that you want to identify (*eg*, gender, age, nationality, experience). Provide a place at the top of the questionnaire to collect this information or use a *Respondent Profile Sheet.*

Decide if you are using closed or open questions, or both. Closed questions ask the respondent to choose from given answers; open questions ask the respondent to write in their replies.

Decide what you want to know. Use your research question and sub-questions.

Write your questions.

Decide how respondents will reply to the questions. For example, you might want to use a Likert rating scale where the respondent chooses a number from 1 to 4: 1 means strongly disagree; 2 means disagree; 3 means agree; 4 means strongly agrees.

Write instructions explaining the rating scale at the top of the questionnaire.

Funnel your questions. Start with the general and move to the more specific.

3. Revise your questionnaire

Pilot (test) your questionnaire using at least three respondents.

Make changes according to the results of the pilot questionnaire. For example, you may want to make a question clearer, add a question, or change your sample if all the respondents answered all the questions the same way. Use *Traps to avoid* to determine whether any of your questions are faulty. Revise faulty questions.

Use *Standards for validity and reliability* to revise questions that do not meet these two standards.

Can your questionnaire be used without help? Edit your questionnaire for readability and clarity.

Do not add new questions after the pilot is administered.

4. Traps to avoid when writing your questions

Double question: Do you walk to school or carry your lunch?

Wrong-choice question: Is your hair yellow, purple, green or blue?

The kitchen sink question: Please list all the schools you have attended, your teachers and what grades you got.

The fuzzy word questions: Should middle-aged people live it up?

The cover the world question: What do you think of racism?

Jargon questions: Do you feel your cognitive and affective domains have been adequately addressed in school?

Dream questions: What kind of education would you like for your child?

Leading questions: Why are you happy here at FIS?

Hearsay questions: Do you think students are happy at FIS?

Assumptions: Why did you choose FIS as your school?

5. Standards for validity and reliability

Validity: Do your questions measure what you want them to measure? Do they produce answers that accurately reflect the respondent's beliefs, experience or situation?

Reliability: Do the questions and answers have consistency and reliability? Consistency: Are the questions and answers consistent and repeatable? Will the same question asked of the same person in similar circumstances produce the same answer? Repeatability: If the same question was asked in different ways, at different points, would the answer be the same?

6. Administer the questionnaire

Get informed consent from each respondent (see *Informed Consent Form*).

You must decide on a method of distributing and collecting the questionnaires that will ensure that you get back as many as possible.

Your return rate could be very low if you leave it to chance. Suggestion: if possible, stay with the respondents while they fill out the questionnaire. If this is not possible, send out twice the number of surveys that you need to be returned.

Stay in control of your sample: do not let anyone participate who has not been chosen for the sample.

7. Suggestions for analysing the data collected from the questionnaires

- **Quantify and categorise (group) data**

  Count the responses for each question or category of questions. For example, if you used the Likert rating scale, count how many people answered 1, 2, 3, and 4 for each question.

  Make a table or graph to display the data. Discuss the results in your paper and include the display.

  Find the mean (average), the mode (the most frequent answer) or the median (the middle answer) for each question, or for questions you want to discuss more fully in your paper. These can also be displayed in a table.

- **Colour code and categorise data**

  Look for patterns or trends (For example, words that have been repeated by several different respondents in open-ended questions) and highlight the words. Use different coloured highlighters for different ideas or categories (groups) of data. Use your sub-questions for ideas for categories. Look for relationships between characteristics of the respondents (age, gender, nationality, experience) in the *Profile* and the responses given.

  Discuss the trends or patterns you observed in the data in your paper. Use quotations as the display of data.

Example of a questionnaire

What do students think about the Grade 10 research paper? Here is your chance to grade us! What did you think of the project? Assign a number to each statement. The highest rating (4) indicates that you agree and the lowest (1) indicates that you disagree.

1. The timelines were reasonable.

        1   2   3   4

2. Instructions were clear.

        1   2   3   4

3. Library resources were adequate.

        1   2   3   4

4. The grading system was fair.

        1   2   3   4

5. The bibliography charts were helpful.

        1   2   3   4

6. The key word list was helpful.

        1   2   3   4

7. Forming a research question and sub-questions was helpful.

        1   2   3   4

8. I felt well prepared to search for information.

        1   2   3   4

9. I could get help when I needed it.

        1   2   3   4

10. I liked using at least one primary method of data collection.

        1   2   3   4

11. I liked using at least one method of analysis.

        1   2   3   4

What do you think?

1. What were the best aspects of this project?
2. What would you change?
3. What was the most difficult task you had? Why was it difficult?
5. How was this research assignment different from the way you have done research in the past?
6. What did you learn that will help you do your Extended Essay next year?
7. Do you think it was worth the class time allotted? Why?

Other Comments?

F2. How to do an interview

What is an interview?

A set of questions presented to a set number of individuals who belong to a sample chosen by the researcher because they know about the topic and/or have the characteristics that will help the researcher make connections or draw conclusions about the research question(s). See attached page for an example of an interview schedule.

Is an interview the best way for you to collect your data?

Do you have 10-20 questions to ask of 3-10 people? (The fewer people, the longer the interviews).

Do you want to compare how answers are the same or different for subsets in your sample (gender, nationality, age, experience).

Do you want to analyse respondents' comments to look for patterns?

Do you want to go into detail and/or investigate more complex or sensitive issues?

How do you do an interview?

1. Select the type of interview you will do from the following interview types:

- **Standardised schedule interview (the interviewer has prepared, written questions)**
  The same information is required of each person and each is asked exactly the same questions in the same order.
  Questions are a type of questionnaire (See *How to do a Questionnaire*)
  Use this type for interviewing a larger number of people.
  Use this type of interviewing for respondents who share the same characteristics or outlooks.
  Data will fall into neat categories for analysis.

- **Standardised interview, no schedule (questions are written as a guide but not strictly followed)**
  Different questions or kinds of questions, perhaps put in a different order, are necessary to get the same information from different people.
  Data will cover more material and will not fall into neat categories.
  Interviewer has a research outline that helps him/her remember the points to be covered.

- **Unstructured interview (no written question or guide since this data is collected at the beginning of the research.) This method is not recommended for beginners.**
  There is no set order of wording of questions, no schedule (written questions).

Different information is needed from different respondents.

Data will cover more material and will not fall into neat categories.

Data will be used for formulating the research question(s) and limiting the research.

2. Write the interview questions

Determine characteristics of your respondents that you want to identify (*eg* gender, age). Provide a place at the top of the questionnaire to collect this information or use a **Respondent profile sheet**.

Decide if you are using an interview schedule (written questions) or a research outlined.

Decide what you want to know. Use your research question and sub-questions. Write your questions.

Funnel your questions. Start with the general and move to the more specific.

3. Revise the interview questions

Pilot (test) your questionnaire using at least two respondents. Tape the interviews.

Listen to the audiotapes.

Make changes according to the results of the pilot interviews. For example, you may want to make a question clearer, or change your sample if all the respondents answered all the questions the same way.

Use *Traps to avoid* to determine whether any of your questions are faulty. Revise faulty questions.

Use *Standards for Validity and Reliability* to revise questions that do not meet these two standards.

Do not add new questions after the pilot, or practise, interview.

4. Traps to avoid when writing your questions (see p156)

5. Standards for validity and reliability (see p156)

6. Conduct the interview

Get informed consent from each respondent (see *Informed Consent Form*).

Introduce yourself and tell the respondent what you are researching, *ie* your research question.

Bring a tape recorder and new tape. Test the recorder.

Establish a friendly but serious tone and *encourage respondents to talk* in your interview. An example follows:

Question: What do you like best about living in this neighbourhood?
Answer: The people.
Question: What is it about the people that you like?

Take notes regarding any physical characteristics (gesturing, facial expressions) that may be relevant.

7. Suggestions for analysing the data from the interviews

- **Transcribe data**

  Play the tapes and type or write the answers for each respondent on a blank interview schedule, if you had structured interviews, or on your research outline if you did not use a schedule. **Listening to the tapes is not enough: you must transcribe them in order to find patterns, trends in the data.**

- **Colour code and categorise data**

  Group the responses for each question or category of questions. For example, colour code all the answers to question 1, make note of characteristics, such as gender, age, *etc* for each answer, then cut and stack answers.

  Look for patterns or trends (for example, words that have been repeated by several different respondents in open-ended questions) and highlight the words. Use different coloured highlighters for different ideas or categories (groups) of data. Use your sub-questions for ideas for categories. Look for relationships between characteristics of the respondents (age, gender, nationality, experience) and the responses given.

  Discuss the trends and patterns of data in your paper. You may use quotations from the interview that are typical of answers or that you think are important. You may develop a model or diagram to display the data.

Sample interview schedule

The following questions were used to interview students who were doing a research paper for Biology. The researcher was trying to find out how they felt about their assignment and whether or not concept mapping affected the way they searched for information. She observed the students while they searched for information and interviewed them as well.

Name of respondent: _____

Day & date: _____

Time questionnaire/interview began: _____

Time questionnaire/interview ended: _____

Concept Mapper: yes   no

1   How is your research going for your Biology paper?

2   If you used a concept map, did you find it helpful?
    Why/Why not?

3   What were you looking for in your search?

4   What is your research topic? Research questions?

5   What is the title of your paper?

6   What are the requirements of the research assignment?

7   Where have you looked for information in the library?

8   Where have you looked for information outside the library?

9   What did you accomplish during your searching?

10 How do you decide when your search is over?

11 Where did you get your search terms?

12 Do you prefer subject heading or key word searching? Why?

13 How do you like the research process we are using for this project?

14 Has anything you learned in class helped you to search? How?

15 How did you decide what to keep and what to discard in your
    searching?

16 Now that you have completed your search, what would you do
    differently? Why?

17 Do you prefer SIRS or the on-line catalogue? Why?

18 What adjectives would you use to describe how you felt when you
    started the search?

19 When you finished? Since the last time you searched? Since the first
    search you did?

20 Did you find enough sources during your search? Too many?

21 How do your first two searches compare with each other? With your
    last two?

22 How do you decide if it is a successful search?

23 Please identify and diagram or describe your best and worst searches.

F3. Example of a respondent profile

It is important that you design your respondent profile to provide the information that will help you analyse your data. Grouping your respondents' answers by gender, age and nationality will help you to discover trends, or patterns, in the data. (For example, do boys always agree with question 1 and girls almost always disagree? In your analysis you will try to find information or other data that point to an explanation.) Other categories for the profile will depend on your research question, what you are looking for, and what connections you suspect might be useful. You can include this profile at the top of your questionnaire or as a separate paper.

Be careful to keep the user profile attached to the respondent's questionnaire or to the transcribed (typed, written) notes you have made from interview tapes.

Gender

      Male   Female

Age

      13   14   15   16   17   18

Country of birth

      English-speaking country

      Non-English speaking country

English

      First language ☐   Second language ☐

Number of schools attended since age 5

      1   2   3   4   5   more than 5

F4. Letter of informed consent

[date]

Dear _____

You are invited to participate in a study that I am doing as a Grade 10 student at _____ International School to investigate the question:

_____

The purpose of the study is to:

_____

As a participant, you will be asked to:

_____

Your responses will be kept confidential, and in no way will you be able to be identified through them. Only the researcher will have access to the information you provide. Should I wish to quote you in my paper, I will get your permission to cite the quotation. If you do not agree, the quote will remain anonymous.

If you agree to participate, please sign and date the form below. Your signature indicates that you have read and understood the information in this letter and that you voluntarily give your informed consent to participate in the study.

Yours truly,

_____

[Name of researcher]

_____

I agree to participate in the study according to the guidelines stated above.

_____

Signature of Participant   Date

G. How do I analyse data?

After collecting data a researcher analyses, or interprets, the data. The method of analysis grows out of the research question and is used as a way of organising data.

G1: Methods of analysis

Method of Analysis: Look for...	What it means	Example of research question or sub-question
Comparing (Similarities)	How are things alike?	How is acupuncture similar to an anaesthetic?
Contrasting (Differences)	How are things different?	How are marriage rites in Far Eastern societies different from those in Western societies?
Constructing support	What is the support for the argument? What are the limitations of it?	Is the universe 'open' (expanding forever) or 'closed' (collapsing on itself?)
Classifying/Labelling (Categories)	How can I put things in groups? What are the rules governing membership in these groups? How can I name the groups?	What is the role of ethnic groups in US political elections?
Structural Analysis (Main idea/supporting evidence)	What is the most central idea? What is the evidence to support what you say about the main idea?	Did John Kennedy mishandle the Cuban Missile Crisis?
Induction	What conclusions, generalisations can you make and what is the support for them?	Are electrons and other sub-atomic particles subject to wave-like behaviour?
Deduction	What is the proof that this must be true?	Is there extraterrestrial life?
Chronology by time or stage	How can I arrange data in time order?	How did Monet's life influence his art?
Pros/Cons	What are the arguments in favour and against a point of view?	Should marijuana be legalised?
Causes/Effects	What were the reasons and results of an event?	What were the causes and effects of the end of the Cold War?
Problems/Solutions	Why doesn't something work and how can we make it work?	What disrupts peace between Israel and Palestine?
Procedures/ Experimental inquiry	What are the steps involved in doing something? What can I observe? How can I describe it, explain it?	How is liquid oxygen produced?
Relationships (Spatial, human)	What does one thing have to do with another?	How have computer graphics influenced contemporary art?

Method of Analysis: Look for...	What it means	Example of research question or sub-question
Analysis	How can a subject be divided into significant parts?	What were the issues related to the U-2 incident?
Literary or artistic themes	What are the themes inherent in works of literature?	What are the recurrent Romantic themes in Wordsworth's poetry?
Spatial	What are the geographic or physical boundaries?	How is oil distributed in the five continents?
Patterns	What is recurring and what is the system or order to the recurrence?	How can alcoholism be defined through observation of a case study?
Invention	How can this be improved? What new thing is needed?	How can a solar energy house be built?
System analysis	How does it operate? How are its parts related?	Can artificial intelligence replace the human brain?
Decision making	What would be best? Worst?	Is arms control a deterrent to war?
Error analysis	What's wrong with this?	Why is the Vietnam War considered an American failure?
Perspectives	What are the reasons for different opinions?	How have professional sports changed for owners, players and fans?
Extending	How can the information be represented in a different way?	How has the incidence of child abuse changed from 1970-90?
Investigation	What are the defining characteristics? Why/how did this happen? What if...?	Is global warming a threat to the planet Earth?
Problem solving	How can an obstacle be overcome?	How can car emissions be reduced?
Statistical description and analysis	How can we use statistics to describe or interpret numerical data to show relationships such as correlation?	How does the discharge vary along the course of River X? What is the mode, median and mean of test scores of Grade 9 students in Maths?

HOW CAN I...

Represent/display it?	Improve it?	Take it apart?
Generalise about it?	Predict what is next?	Determine what's wrong?
Look at it differently?	Put it together?	Explain it?
Imagine what if?	Fix or overcome it?	Solve it
Make connections?	Classify, categorise it?	
Define it?	Find exceptions?	

G2: Asking analytical questions

In search of a question ongoing analysis

LOOK FOR...	HOW CAN I...

LOOK FOR...

- **Chronological order/stages**
- **Procedures/steps**
- **Causes/effects**
- **Problems/solutions**
- **Similarities/differences**
- **Relationships (human/spatial)**
- **Themes (Literary/artistic)**
- **Pros/cons**
- **Main ideas/supporting evidence**
- **Patterns**
- **Perspectives**
- **Best-worst/Most-least**
- **Connections**
- **Defining characteristics**
- **How it works**

HOW CAN I...

- **represent/display data?**
- **classify/categorize?**
- **generalize?**
- **find exceptions?**
- **predict what is next?**
- **imagine what if...?**
- **determine what's wrong?**

H. Project evaluation of the 10th Grade research paper

See F1. *How to do a questionnaire or survey-example of a questionnaire*

Recommended web sites

Exemplars of 10th Grade Student Research Papers
http://www.ecis.org

Action research

Students as Authentic Researchers: A New Prescription for the High School
Research Paper
http://www.ecis.org

School Services Center: What is Action Research?
http://www.ael.org/rel/schlserv/action.htm

Teacher as Researcher
http://www.ed.gov/databases/ERIC_Digests/ed355205.html

Chapter Eight

Putting the Learner in Charge: Is Information Literacy Enough?

Activity:	The Independent Project
Level:	Grades 9, 10
Interdisciplinary Action:	All subjects
Information Literacy Focus:	Personal management, organisational skills
Project Designers:	Andrew MacDonald, Frankfurt International School, Steve Castledine, Istanbul International Community School, Carol Gordon

Project description

All students in the grade participate in this unit. Designed to help students become independent learners, it is appropriate for ninth or tenth grade. Authentic learning tasks/assessments are structured to give students feedback on their performance and consistent, one-to-one adult support. Students, working alone or in a group of two or three, plan and create a project that can be a production, composition, work of art or literature, experiment, model, computer program or presentation that conveys a message to the audience (*ie*, viewer or listener.) The outcome cannot be a written paper. Students record process and progress in their journals, including notes and a bibliography chart for the research component of the project, two proposals that focus the project with a statement of what the project will look like. The culmination of the unit is an exhibition.

Projects evolve from students' personal interests and backgrounds. Culturally based projects are encouraged. Adaptation of the unit for ESL students includes doing the project in their primary language with the following guidelines:

Students choose an advisor who speaks the primary language of the student.

The advisor may not normally be a parent or relative of the student.

Feedback, commentary is from parents who speak the native tongue of the student and English.

The following examples of independent projects help students generate ideas for projects:

A play production showing the experiences of an asylum seeker in Germany.

A design for a beach chair-trolley accompanied by a feasibility or marketing study and proposal for manufacture and distribution.

A webzine piece on teenage fashions.

An investigation of your town's sports facilities for people with physical handicaps and a proposal for a community-wide recreational programme.

An analysis of how fourth year students develop language skills through a series of lessons taught to second graders.

Models of Korean temples.

A Japanese meal.

An original musical composition in the style of Chopin.

The unit is six weeks in length, running parallel to school routine and activities. It is extra curricular in the sense that it is not embedded in scheduled classes. This presents the challenge of convening the grade level during lunch times, activity periods, homeroom time, or in an assembly. Large group activities occur three times in six weeks: 1) introduction and orientation to the project, including distribution and explanation of the student packet; 2) a peer review session mid-way through the unit; 3) a planning session for the Exhibition.

The librarian, Head of the English Department and grade level adviser manage the unit. This will vary with organisational structure and staffing in each school. Students choose an adviser from school staff, their community, church or families; parents, siblings and other students are not eligible.

The unit applies authentic assessment techniques that include rubrics for self-evaluation and adviser in-put, journals and peer review. A final assessment of the project takes place at the Exhibition. Teams, each consisting of two assessors, visit each project. The teams use student-written rubrics to assess the product and student journals to assess process.

The final assessment is a short narrative report that becomes part of the students' academic records.

The learning objectives of the independent project are:

1. Personal Management: How to be a successful researcher/implementer and develop skills in:

    Planning

    Organising events

    Problem-solving

    Decision-making

    Meeting deadlines

    Managing materials

    Self assessing

2. Working with Others

    Establishing communication with an adviser

    Working cooperatively with peers and collaborators

Support materials (p181-190)

A.   Student packet

A1.   Proposal for Grade 9 independent project

A2.   Sample calendar/planner

A3.   The Journal – sample of a student journal; journal entries sheet

A4.   Memo to solicit advisers

A5.   Adviser response sheet

Evaluation of student achievement

A. The Journal

See Support materials, A3 (p184)

The journal drew from the follow checklist of suggestions:

Continuous feedback (oral, written) from advisor with reference to the journal.

Self-assessment using the Journal Checklist.

Planner: A calendar with tasks, meetings, deadlines.

Information/data gathered from resources (notes).

Bibliography chart.

States problems, decisions, changes in plan, collaboration, use of resources, solutions.

Keeps track of progress through writing, photographs, sketches.
Ongoing self-assessment: How am I doing?

B. Peer review using PQP

Directions: Discuss your project with your partner. Allow your partner to use your proposal and assessment criteria to give you feedback on how well you are doing.

PRAISE (What are the strengths of the project? Be specific: refer to the proposal and assessment criteria.)
QUESTIONS (What helpful questions would you like to ask about the project? What problems do you see with the project?)
POLISH (What suggestions do you have to solve the problems or improve the project?)

Reviewed for: _____

Reviewed by: _____

C. Independent project assessment criteria for personal management: rubric for self-evaluation

1. Using evidence from your proposal, calendar planner, journal, bibliography charts and any other documentation you have kept, summarise the processes you went through to answer the following questions.

2. Write a narrative in the boxes below using specific evidence to evaluate how well you did in each category.

3. Give yourself a rating from 1 to 5; 5 being the highest that represents how well you did in each category.

4. Talk to your adviser about your self-assessment to see if he/she agrees with your assessment of your personal management skills.

Rubric for self-evaluation

RESEARCH PROCESS	PERSONAL NARRATIVE	MY RATING	ADVISER'S RATING
PLANNING • What message did I want my project to give? Did I succeed? • What did I expect to learn? • Did I accomplish my goals? (Proposal)			
MEETING DEADLINES • How well did I manage my time? (Calendar)			
ORGANISATION • How well did I gather information from reading, note taking and talking to people? • How did I manage the materials and tools I needed? (See Bibliography Chart) • How did I organise my exhibition? (Journal)			
WORKING WITH ADVISER • Did I ask questions and seek help when I needed it? • Did I take initiative to set up meetings? (Journal, Calendar)			
PROBLEM SOLVING Decision making • What problems did I face and how did I solve them? • What decisions did I make? (Journal)			

D. Independent project: assessment criteria for project and exhibition

1. Choose two ways to evaluate your project and two ways to evaluate your exhibition.
2. Write a narrative that explains how your project/exhibition met these criteria.
3. Give yourself a rating from 1 to 5; 5 being the highest, that represents how well you did in each category.
4. Talk to your adviser about your self-assessment to see he/she agrees with your assessment of your project and exhibition.

Assessment criteria for project and exhibition

	PERSONAL NARRATIVE	MY RATING	ADVISER'S RATING
PROJECT CRITERIA			
1 (Example: My project sent the message I intended for my audience)			
2 (Example: In doing my project I overcame an important obstacle)			
EXHIBITION CRITERIA			
1 (Example: My exhibit had an introduction, a good explanation of how I did the project, and a conclusion)			
2 (Example: In performing my exhibition I spoke clearly and with confidence)			

E. Adviser's narrative for the student record

This evaluation was made by two assessors and was based on a 15 minute interview with the student during the independent project exhibition, the student's journal entries and the standards identified in the rubric assessment criteria for project and exhibition.

Name of student

Title of project

Student's abstract

Assessors' narrative

Assessor   Assessor

Reflection

The Role of the librarian in teaching independent learning

The scope of information literacy, expanded to include emotional intelligence, sets a new agenda for librarians to define the prerequisite skills for independent learning. An independent learning project addresses self-management skills in a context that is motivating by virtue of the elective nature of topic selection and extra curricular design. However, this model is one of many possible models. Developmental appropriateness and individual differences suggest that elements of this model could be integrated with traditional, academic assignments that address cognitive facets of information literacy. An independent learning project, in part or whole, recurring at various grade levels, can provide archival material to track growth and progress, for which the use of the portfolio, another powerful authentic assessment instrument, is indicated. Ninth graders could use what they have learned about themselves as independent learners to re-visit other resource-based projects that have been stored in their cumulative portfolios. Reflective entries that address, 'How I would do this differently now' are useful exercises in metacognitive, learning how to learn, thinking.

Porfolios and other authentic learning and assessment tools can help the librarians to highlight information literacy, for teachers and students, as an important component of the process of learning. Authentic methods are particularly well-suited to promoting emotional intelligence because they assess process, yet accommodate evaluation of product and presentation. Crafting lessons and units with journal writing, rubrics, peer reviews, and self-evaluations, puts the librarian in the position of a leader or mentor in instructional design and puts the student in charge of his or her own learning. Librarians can use performance-based strategies for articulation, both horizontally across curriculum, and vertically, through the upper grades.

The backbone of the *Independent Project* is the journal, an authentic assessment tool that directs the student's attention to progress and process. It provides the opportunity for dialogue as teachers and/or librarians respond to student entries. An electronic form of the journal, email, can be a useful way for librarians to establish and maintain contact with students while they are working through various stages of the research process.

The librarian can be a powerful liaison between school and community. The involvement of family and community in advisement and assessment roles makes one-on-one contact feasible, affording students personal attention and sustained discourse, which emerged from this study as stimulants for metacognitive thinking and self-reflection. The performance-based independent project model strengthens ties between school and community and helps parents to understand how they can support educators' goals for information literacy and independent learning.

Implicit in this project is the role of the librarian as a facilitator. Rather than teaching emotional intelligence and metacogntive thinking, she creates opportunities for students to learn them. In fact, this is true of most of information literacy instruction. She generates and manages project work in an exemplary way, as a proactive, rather than reactive, agent. The performance-based design is an instrument for teaching the entire community of learners: administrators, parents as well as other teachers. Action research, as a component of the instructional design, promotes reflective practice among colleagues. The librarian is seen as a researcher and role model. She is perceived as truly concerned with the process of learning.

To access the action research study, *Independent Learning: Can It Be Taught?* go to **http://www.ecis.org**

Support Materials
for Chapter Eight

A. Sample student packet – front page

Grade 9 Independent Project

IMA Student
ABC International School
March-May 2001

A1. Proposal for Grade 9 independent project

Due Date:
Student:
Adviser:
Title of Project:

Purpose	**Outcome**
a. What exactly do you want to achieve in your project?	a. What will your audience (listeners, viewers) be able to see and/or hear?
b. What do you expect to learn about yourself?	b. What exactly will your display, exhibit, presentation for the May 28th Exhibition consist of?
Resources	**Problem solving**
a. What materials, equipment do you need?	a. What problems do you think you will have?
b. What will your costs be?	
	b. How can you overcome these problems?
c. To whom might you talk, apart from your advisor?	

Approved by Adviser _____ on _____
[name]   Date
Approved by Steering Committee _____ on _____
[names of teachers/librarian]   Date

A2. Sample calendar/planner

Month One

Monday	Tuesday	Wednesday	Thursday	Friday	Saturday	Sunday
2	3	4	5	6	7	8
9	10	11 Introduction for students 14:00 Auditorium	12 Orientation for advisers 15:15 19:00 Room 311	13 Students select adviser	14 Students select adviser	15 Students select adviser
16	17	18 Students select adviser	19 Students select adviser	20 Students select adviser	21	22
23 Deadline for proposal signed by adviser	24	25	26 Deadline for proposals to Steering Committee via the library	27	28	29
30	31					

Planners should be provided for a three month period. Month two planner should give a date when the assessment criteria are due to the adviser – usually four weeks after the deadline for proposals. Month three planner will show:

a. where and when the peer review session will take place – usually two weeks after the assessment criteria;
b. when the project is due – two weeks after (a);
c. day and time of the exhibition, which is then followed by the assessment – one week after (b).

A3. The Journal

The Journal:

A story of the progress of my project

Hints for good journal entries:

1. Date each entry

2. Include written narrative, audiotapes, photographs, sketches, timelines, notes, calculations, checklists of things to do, and any other evidence of organisation and progress.

3. Include plans to set up and break down your exhibit, including diagrams if appropriate. Remember that you have 20 minutes for each.

4. Individualise your journal so it reflects your personality and the uniqueness of your project.

You may use the sheets in this packet, adding more as needed, or you may buy or make your own journal.

Sample of a student journal

27 April

I want my independent project to be something I am really interested in since I will be working on it for the next month. It seems to me I should think about two things:

1) What I am curious about or what do I want to learn more about and be able to do?

2) What do I want the outcome to look like? When I think of the exhibition and what I will present as my project, I immediately think of doing something with drama. I really liked being in the Middle School play last year and I am also interested in young children, so it might be a good idea to talk to an elementary teacher about putting on a play with some children from his or her class. It seems like a big job and I really don't know where to start.

30 April

I went to the Elementary library to see what plays they had for young children and found two possibilities. Mrs M suggested I look in the Middle/High Library as well. I also found some books that contained one act plays and skits. Perhaps it is more realistic to do a shorter piece rather than an whole play. I asked Mrs M if she could recommend an elementary teacher and she told me to talk to Mrs L who teaches 5th grade and German. I had another idea today to use my German language in this project. Perhaps I will meet with an elementary German teacher who could give me some advice.

4 May

I met with Mrs L and we talked about my idea. She gave me some things to read that might be good scripts. We talked about the date for my exhibition and inviting the parents to come to the event. Right now I feel as though I have to make the decision about the play. Mrs L suggested that I come to her class and let the students have input into the decision. I think this is a good idea, but I should give them some choices so we can come to a decision by the end of the class-time. I really need to make a calendar with some deadlines so that I am sure to finish my project on time. I am working on the first draft of my proposal that I will complete when I have an adviser.

5 May

I was talking with my friend, Susan, about her project. She is interested in re-writing fairy tales to show how they used stereotypes. I think this might be a good idea from my play. Susan has agreed to come to the class with me to talk about it. I called Mrs L and she said that sounded like a good idea. I asked Mrs L to be my adviser and she said yes. I also gave her the materials she needs to have for the independent project and she said she would come to the training session for it. I am ready to write my proposal and hand it in for approval. She looked at my proposal and we filled in some of the gaps. Now I feel like I know what I am doing!

6 May

Susan and I visited Mrs L's class and her students liked Susan's stories. I am worried that Susan hasn't finished her book and we still have to write dialogue for the play. Susan and I talked about this and she agreed to a deadline. Meanwhile, I am going to choose something that is already written just in case. We will dramatize three stories that are based on German fairy tales. The play will be in both English and German. Mrs L and I will choose the cast after students audition for parts.

8 May

I have done my calendar with deadlines and given a copy to my adviser. She suggested a few changes and we agreed that rehearsals would take place during her class time. We discussed casting the characters and scheduled auditions. One problem that occurred is that we do not have enough characters to involve the whole class. We decided to create some non-acting roles for students who would be more comfortable creating scenery, organising props, making masks and putting together simple costumes, doing sound effects, making a programme and cue cards.

12 May

Rehearsals are going well but one student has not memorised his lines and seems very shy about performing in front of others. I talked with Mrs L and she suggested that we give him a choice of other jobs and cast Jonathan in the role.

Sample abstract

The play, *Fairy Tales Grimm* dramatised three tales adapted by Sandra Wilson from *Grimm's Fairy Tales*. The cast of characters was drawn from Mrs L's fifth-grade German class and involved ten students. Ten other students were involved in mask making, props, design of the programme, cue cards and publicity. The play was 15 minutes long and consisted of the following three scenes: 'The Twelve Dancing Princes', 'Hansel and Gretel' and 'Snow White and Red Rose.' The traditional stories were humorous adaptations that were re-written to point out the use of stereotypes in children's fairy tales.

Provide sheets of lined paper for journal entries in the student packet.

A4. Sample memo to solicit advisers

An Invitation to share your talents:
The Grade Nine independent project

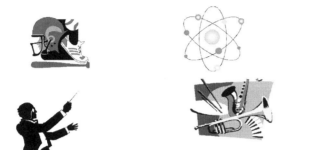

What is an independent project?

The outcome may be a production, composition, work of art or literature, experiment, model, computer program or presentation that conveys a message to the audience *ie*, viewer or listener. The outcome cannot be a written paper based on secondary sources.

What does an adviser do?

1 Attends a one-hour training session on [date] at 15:30 or 19:00 at school which will specify requirements, tasks, deadlines and outcomes.

2 Meets or talks with the student when needed, providing practical advice.

3 Attends the exhibition on [date].

4 Writes a short narrative for the student's record that describes and comments on the project.

5 Advises the student for a maximum total of five hours.

Why are we doing independent projects in Ninth Grade?

The objectives of the independent project are pastoral: we are cultivating in students those qualities that will help them to be successful in their academic and personal lives. The emphasis is on personal management: planning and organising an event, problem-solving, decision making, meeting deadlines, managing materials, and being critics of their own work. Other goals include communicating successfully and working with an adviser, and with other people who will become part of the desired outcome. Students may choose to do their project in their native language with the following guidelines:

1 They choose an adviser who speaks their *native tongue and English.*
2 The adviser may *not normally be a parent or relative.*
3 Feedback, commentary is from advisers who speak their native tongue.

A5. Sample adviser response sheet

Grade Nine independent project

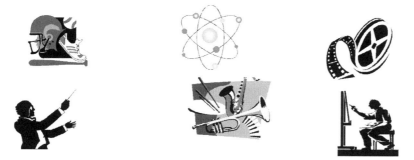

I would like to put my name forward to advise a 9th Grade student for his/her independent project

Name_____

Home Phone _____

I can offer advice, expertise, and/or experience in the following areas:

_____

_____

_____

_____

Recommended web sites

Authentic Assessment Bibliography
http://www.sccoe.k12.ca.us/authasse.htm

ECIS Web Site - Putting the Learner in Charge: Are Information Literacy
Skills Enough?
http://www.ecis.org

Integration of the Disciplines in Authentic Assessment
http://www.orst.edu/instruction/ed555/zone5/zone5hom.htm

Chapter Nine

Buckets of Books

Activity One: Forty novel ideas

Level: Grades 5-10

Interdisciplinary Action: English/language arts, modern
                                    languages

Information Literacy Focus: Reading for pleasure

Project Designer: Carol Gordon

Project description

Literary response and choice are key factors in reading motivation. A generous list of response activities from which students can choose is a viable alternative to 'the book report' and worksheets that target the facts, rather than the aesthetic and thematic elements of a book. These choices invite learners to respond in verbal, kinaesthetic, musical, mathematical, and artistic modes. Students may choose to work alone or with a partner. English teachers may use this list throughout the year. The librarian supplies books, delivered in colourful buckets by students who take turns selecting titles from the library. Books are checked out to the English teacher. Having an abundance of books in classrooms, surrounded by the annotated reading lists, will personalise the project as students choose books from their 'own' classroom library.

Support materials

Forty novel ideas

1   Record a telephone conversation with your friend as you discuss how the main character resembles someone you know.

2   Plan a dinner party for a character that is consistent with his or her personality. Write instructions to the catering staff, including the menu, table setting and guest list of celebrities.

3   Write a song or letter that describes your feelings about a character beginning with the sentence, 'I was (your verb) by ...'

4   Draw a timeline that shows the chronology of events in the life of one character. Add details to those from the book to further develop the character.

5   Prepare to interview the main character by writing five interview questions then write the answers you think the character would give. Tape the interview.

6   Write an epilogue and/or prologue to the book, describing events that could have taken place before and after the plot of the book.

7   Take photographs and make a photo album that depicts the experiences of a character.

8   Pretend you are casting the characters to play in the movie version of the book and list the actors and actresses you would choose and why.

9   Write a eulogy for the funeral of the main character.

10 Pretend you are a travel agent and plan a vacation for a character, supplying all the necessary documents, reservations, tickets, itinerary, travel brochures and any other information that your character will need.

11 Design a wardrobe for the main character and make drawings or paper dolls.

12 Draw a map of the main setting of the book, labelling important locations.

13 Write a letter to the author; ask questions you are curious about and explain your reaction to his/her book.

14 Brainstorm other titles for the book and design illustrated bookmarks that relate to each of the titles.

15 Pretend you are a librarian; write a explanation of why you chose this book for the school library. (You may interview the librarian to get ideas.)

16 Pretend you're the author and explain why you wrote the book and how you chose the title, setting and created the characters.

17 Research the life of the author and make a chart that shows how the book reflects the author's life.

18 Pretend you are the author and write a speech accepting an award for the book.

19 Change the setting (time and/or place) of the book and illustrate the

main events of the story and the characters.

20 Design and create a cover for the book that illustrates an interesting scene or that captures the book's theme.

21 Design and create a calendar that depicts the events of the book.

22 Pretend you are from another century and you found this book in a time capsule. Make a list of questions would you have about the characters, setting and events in the book.

23 Describe what you think happened to the main character after the book ended.

24 Explain why your book should be included in a capsule to be dug up in 100 years.

25 Make a mind map of the book and compare it with a mind map of another book you have read.

26 Describe an experience you've had that was like the experience of the character.

27 Compare the book with a movie or TV programme of the same kind.

28 Write an advertisement for the book.

29 Write 10 discussion questions for the book.

30 Pretend you are a famous movie star who has been asked to play a character. Explain why you want to do the role.

31 Write a TV commercial for the book.

32 Make a TV script for one scene of your book.

33 Pretend you are movie director and videotape your 'pitch' as you try to sell your ideas about making this book into a movie to a producer.

34 Pretend you are a doctor or lawyer. Give advice to a character from the book who has a medical or legal problem.

35 Write a different ending for the book.

36 Keep a journal as you read the book that includes your reactions, thoughts, feelings.

37 Write a five-line 'easy' poem abut your book: a noun, then two adjectives, then three verbs, then a thought about the noun, and finally a synonym for the noun.

38 Write two articles for a newspaper published at the time of or in the country of your book relating an important event from two different points of view, or relate two different events from the book.

39 Write a diary pretending you are your favourite character in the book.

40 Write and illustrate a dictionary that includes the unique words in this book.

Activity Two:	Reading workshop
Level:	Grades 5-10
Interdisciplinary Action:	English/language arts, modern languages
Information Literacy Focus:	Reading for interpretation and appreciation
Project Designer:	Carol Gordon

Project description

Reading Workshop, described in Nancie Atwell's book, *In the Middle: Writing, Reading, and Learning with Adolescents*, is a landmark work for English/Language Arts teachers. An understanding of how Reading Workshop is different from other reading programmes is a first step for developing library support for this ongoing reading initiative.

Students complete a reading survey on the first day of school that identifies the types of books they like to read. A follow-up workshop begins with a mini-lesson, *eg*, reading a poem or talking about an author. Each student is expected to maintain a journal in a spiral notebook. Choosing books to read during workshop is also a mini-lesson topic. At the core of Reading Workshop is the active involvement of students as readers of other's writing. Reading is a meaning-seeking process.

Reading Workshop champions independent reading and literary responses that are recorded in journals. Rules for using Reading Workshop time are as follows:

1   Students must read for the entire period.

2   They cannot do homework or read any material for another course. Reading Workshop is not a study hall.

3   They must read a book (no magazines or newspapers where text competes with pictures), preferably one that tells a story (*eg*, novels, histories and biographies rather than books of lists or facts where readers can't sustain attention, build up speed and fluency, or grow to love good stories).

4   They must have a book in their possession when the bell rings; this is the main responsibility involved in coming prepared to this class. (Students who need help finding a book or who finish a book during the workshop are obvious exceptions).

5   They may not talk to or disturb others.

6   They may sit or recline wherever they'd like as long as feet don't go up on furniture and rule #5 is maintained. (A piece of paper taped over the window in the classroom door helps cut down on the number of passers-by who require explanations about students lying around with their noses in books.)

7   There are no lavatory or water fountain sign-outs to disturb me or other readers. In an emergency, they may simply slip out and slip back in again as quietly as possible.

8   A student who's absent can make up time and receive points by reading at home, during study hall (with a note from a parent or study hall teacher), or after school.

Support materials

How can the librarian support Reading Workshop? Here are some strategies:

1   Supply circulation statistics (*The Top Ten Books of the Month*) to English teachers for their mini-lessons on reading.

2   Provide a generous lending policy and large plastic buckets for selected students to transport books they have chosen for their classroom collections.

3   Donate worn paperbacks and duplicates, including gifts and donations, to classroom libraries.

4   Photograph students during Reading Workshop and hang the enlarged photos in the hallways to give reading a high profile.

5   Photograph teachers with their favourite books and frame them as READ posters.

6   Post excerpts from students' journals in the library, with student permission, as promotions for various book titles.

7   Supply annotated bibliographies that are thematic, or that feature the books of an author, for a classroom bulletin-board. Provide lots of extra copies for students to peruse when they are choosing books to read.

8   Schedule classes to visit the library and talk about books as a pre-activity to a mini-lesson.

9   Create electronic bibliographies through the library catalogue or a web page that can be accessed by students who are making book choices.

10 Assist the English teacher in creating a Reading Workshop web page that posts student responses and recommendations for books they have read.

11 Provide a list of literary responses, such as *Forty Novel Ideas*, to stimulate students' journal writing.

12 Plan a book fair, such as *Book Fair with a Flair* described in this chapter, at times that coincide with Reading Workshop and collect student requests for titles.

13 Share recommended web sites, found at the end of this chapter, with students and teachers.

14 Publish newsletters, reading lists and lists of web sites for parents.

15 Conduct discussion groups for parents about books for children and young adults.

Evaluation of student achievement

The journal is the evaluation instrument for this activity. It also serves as a vehicle for the teacher to interact with students and guide their reading choices. Book reports and tests that quiz students' ability to retain factual information about a book are counter-productive to Reading Workshop. Engagement in reading is the goal and only the student can assess whether or not that has happened.

Librarians can monitor circulation statistics during the weeks of Reading Workshop and provide teachers with this data to share with students. This kind of feedback illustrates the library's support for the programme and encourages students to use the library.

Activity Three:	Good things come in threes
Level:	Grades 5-10
Interdisciplinary Action:	English/language arts
Information Literacy Focus:	Reading for understanding and interpretation
Project Designer:	Carol Gordon

Project description

Students choose to read three books by the same author. This ongoing project can be done as a Reading Workshop or as independent reading, or both. In any case, students keep a journal to record their reading responses. They research the life of the author and read at least one article of literary criticism. Library time is scheduled for this activity. Students create projects that illustrate plots, characters, settings or themes (see **Forty novel ideas**) and projects are displayed in the library.

Support materials

This project pre-supposes a strong Young Adult literature section of the library. A survey or circulation records are good instruments to determine which authors are widely read by students. If the library collection is limited, the project can be staggered so that only one class participates at a time. A list of authors, provided by the English teacher and Librarian, ensures that books will be available. This list is compiled with reference to *Authors and Illustrators for Young Adults* and/or *Something About the Author* to ensure that biographical and literary information is available. Photocopying from these sources (observing fair use guidelines) and creating a file in the library will ensure that students can access the articles they need using a photograph of the author on the cover; and arranging each article in a booklet that features one author helps students to relate to the author as a person who is telling a story.

Activity Four:	Book fair with a flair
Level:	Grades 5-10
Interdisciplinary Action:	English/language arts, art
Information Literacy Focus:	Reading for enjoyment
Project Designer:	Carol Gordon

Project description

Book fairs have become staple parts of library programme, bringing books and people together. They are opportunities to celebrate the joy of reading. They can be celebrations that go beyond reading to spotlight talents in a community of learners. When students enter the library to consider their book purchases, they also view exhibits of books, paintings, sculpture, and crafts created by members of staff. Teachers impersonate Charles Dickens and Jane Austen, visiting classrooms in character and costume to perform dramatic readings. A teacher talks about her bike tour through Europe and how she wrote a book about it. Dickens and Shakespeare recite their prose and poetry and Scrooge re-enacts *A Christmas Carol*. Each day of the fair students have sustained silent reading in their English classes. Teacher-musicians perform at a reception for staff in the library as the fair draws to an end.

The book fair becomes an act of discovery. Students see their teachers and other members of staff as actors, musicians and artists. Reading is put in the context of aesthetic appreciation of many art forms.

The support materials in this chapter are intended for the librarian, rather than the students. The following materials are actual communications with staff.

Support materials (p201-206)

A. Sample form soliciting participation of staff members.

B. Sample form asking teachers to sign up for events.

C. Sample schedule of events.

D. Sample schedule confirmation form.

E. Sample evaluation of the event.

Reflection
Reading as a personal process

Student engagement in the reading process is a complex activity that goes beyond an 'assignment'. Our reading preferences and the place reading takes in our lives are deeply personal. Atwell's comments on the nature of reading invite educators to respect the life of the mind.

> When we invite readers' minds to meet books in our classrooms, we invite the messiness of human response – personal prejudices, personal tastes, personal habits, personal experience. But we also invite personal meaning, and the distinct possibility that our kids will grow up to become a different kind of good reader, an adult for whom reading is a logical, satisfying, life-long habit someone who just plain loves books and reading. A new set of priorities for the secondary English curriculum emerges. Pleasure. Fluency. Involvement. Appreciation. Initiative. At its center are readers' responses – to the world of the book, to their own world, to the world-wide, literate community of which they become members, to the meanings they make and re-make as they read. If we revise our portrait of the good reader to fit reality, the first thing we might notice is that he isn't so sure of himself or his texts after all. Whenever he opens a book he accepts an invitation to forge and explore new meanings.
>
> (Atwell, 1987, p. 154)

Reading does not always require a grade. Reading is not a competitive sport. Progress and engagement in reading can be monitored, rather than measured. Evidence of progress can be culled from the students themselves as they record observations about their progress and self-evaluate in their journals. It is more useful to evaluate the progress of each student over time rather than to compare one student to another. Portfolios and journals are excellent assessment tools for providing this kind of feedback.

References

Atwell, N (1987), *In the Middle: Writing, Reading and Learning with Adolescents*, Portsmouth, NH: Heinemann.

Support Materials
for Chapter Nine

Actvity Four: Book fair with a flair

Information Literacy Focus: Reading for enjoyment

A. Form soliciting participation of staff members

BOOK FAIR WITH A FLAIR: EVENTS AND DISPLAYS

Dear Colleagues

A. I would like to present an event for the Fair (a reading, an author impersonation, a musical performance).

Your Name: _____

Name of Event: _____

Length of time of event (maximum 15 minutes): _____

Descriptive statement of event: _____

_____

Periods you are available: _____

[date] _____

[date] _____

If there are enough events we will extend the Fair through Friday so please indicate your availability for [date] _____

B. I would like to display my books, crafts or art work at the fair.

Name _____

Description of exhibit: _____

_____

Please return to [librarian] by [date].

B. Sample form asking teachers to sign up for events

BRINGING BOOKS TO LIFE:
The Book Fair

Dear English Teachers,

Attached please find the programme of events for the Book Fair on [date]. These events will take place in the Student Lounge area or in your classrooms, if you prefer. Classes may attend the Book Fair in the library immediately after their scheduled event.

Please indicate which events you would like for your classes. Use 1, 2 and 3 to indicate your first, second and third choices. I have indicated times rather than periods because of the discrepancies in Middle and High School periods to make it possible to book across divisions. There is flexibility in the starting times of each event. I will try to accommodate your requests and book the events you specify for at least one event.

Sustained Silent Reading, possibly using books purchased at the Fair, is a suggested activity that can take place in homeroom or any subject class during the Book Fair dates to heighten students' awareness of our focus on reading.

The exhibits of teachers' artwork and writings may be viewed at any time in the library but classes should be booked to avoid overcrowding. You may want to construct writing response activities for your students around these exhibits or around the events themselves.

We hope you will all be able to attend the reception for staff in the library on [date] at [time].

Attached are some additional materials about the events that you may find useful for promoting reading with your students, especially during the time of the Book Fair.

[Name of Librarian]

C. Sample schedule of events

A draft of the schedule illustrates how information about the events and performances is disseminated to staff with requests for their input. Gathering information about staff's priorities and preferences is critical to scheduling. Most events are offered by teachers. Sustained Silent Reading is included in the week's events.

Events [Name of event; presenter; time; synopsis]	Priority: 1, 2 or 3	Circle preferred dates and times	Write preferences for length, venue & content
'Biking Through Europe' NS 15 minutes NS tells why and how she wrote her biking books		[Days/times given given in this column]	
'Jane Austen Reads from her Works' KS 15 minutes			
'Kalahari Surfing' TB 15 minutes TB will evoke images of Africa from his book, *Blood Orange*			
'The Tiresome Bard: Sleepy Scenes and Visions from Shakespeare' MP 15-25 minutes Performance of scenes from Shakespeare's plays.			
'Bah, Humbug' MP 15-25 minutes Dramatic reading from Dickens' *A Christmas Carol*			
'Autobiography of a Stranger' KB 15-25 minutes conversation about becoming people with stories to tell.			
Sustained Silent Reading			

D. Schedule confirmation form

BRINGING BOOKS TO LIFE:
The Book Fair

Dear Staff,

Attached please find the schedule of events for the Middle/High School Book Fair on [date]. Please check to see that the schedule is correct:

a.   for those events you have booked for presenters to visit your classes.

b.   for those sessions that you are presenting.

Please note that in some cases smaller classes of students have been combined with larger classes.

English teachers please make your bookings for class visits to the book fair with me to avoid overcrowding and remember to remind your students to bring money should they wish to purchase books. If you would like to bring ten students or fewer you do not need to book a time.

We hope that you will be able to attend the reception in the Library on [date]. Beverages and snacks will be served and we have events planned that celebrate our staff's talents in music, art, literature and drama.

Thank you all for your support,
[Name of Librarian].

Recommended web sites

100 Most Owned Books
http://www.oclc.org/news/oclc/press/19991005a.htm

Asian American, Asian & Pacific Islands Children's Book Awards
http://falcon.jmu.edu/~ramseyil/mulasia.htm

Australian Children's Book Awards
http://www.acs.ucalgary.ca/~dkbrown/austawards.html

BUBL/5:15
http://bubl.ac.uk/link/c/children'sliterature.htm

Canadian Children's Book Awards
http://www.acs.ucalgary.ca/~dkbrown/canawards.html

Canadian Children's Lit Service
http://www.nlc-bnc.ca/services/eelec.htm

Carol Hurst's Children's Literature Site
http://www.carolhurst.com/

Centre for Children's Literature
http://www.macabees.ab.ca./alpha-a.html

Children's Book Council Online
http://www/cbcbooks.org/

Children's Literature
http://www.childrenslit.com/

Children's Literature and Language Arts Resource Menu
http://falcon.jmu.edu/~ramseyil/childlit.htm

The Children's Literature Web Guide
http://www.ucalgary.ca/~dkbrown/

Database of Award-Winning Children's Literature
http://www2.wcoil.com/~ellerbee/childlit.html

A Guide to Children's Literature and Disability
http://www.kidsource.com/NICHCY/literature.html

International Reading Association
http://www.reading.org

Kay Vandergrift's Literature Page
http://www.scils.rutgers.edu/special/kay/childlit.html

References

Brevik, P (1985), Putting libraries back in the information society, *American Libraries*, 16 (10), 723.

Irving, A (1985), *Study and information skills across the curriculum*, Portsmouth, NH: Heinemann.

Joyce, M Tinkham, R, & Trainor, D (1993), *An interdisciplinary approach to teaching the research process using information technology*, Maine Center for Educational Services, (ERIC Document Reproduction Service No. ED 364 248).

Milbury, P (1998), *Problem-based learning, primary sources, and information literacy*, Multimedia Schools, 5, (4), 40-44.

Patterson, J H & Smith, M S (1986), *Meeting the challenge: Computers and higher order thinking*. Madison, WI: Wisconsin Center for Education Research (ERIC Document Reproduction Service No. ED 286 467).

Torp, L & Sage, S (1998), *Problems as possibilities: Problem-based learning in K-12 education*, Alexandria, VA: Association for Supervision and Curriculum Development.